"*Caught* is brutally honest, captivating and hilarious. Nichols puts a focus on several significant problems that could well determine the future of our beloved striped bass."

Mike Laptew, Director, Editor and Producer of *Stripers Gone Wild* and *Secrets of the Striper Pros*

"There's nothing to carp over in this whale of a book. Never once does Nichols flounder as he debones the commercial fishing industry."

Laurence Leamer, Author *Madness Under the Royal Palms: Love and Death Behind the Gates of Palm Beach*

The term addiction is used to describe a recurring compulsion by an individual to engage in some specific activity, despite harmful consequences, as deemed by the user themselves to their individual health, mental state, or social life.

From Wikipedia

Caught

One Man's Maniacal Pursuit of a Sixty Pound Striped Bass and His Experiences with the Black Market Fishing Industry

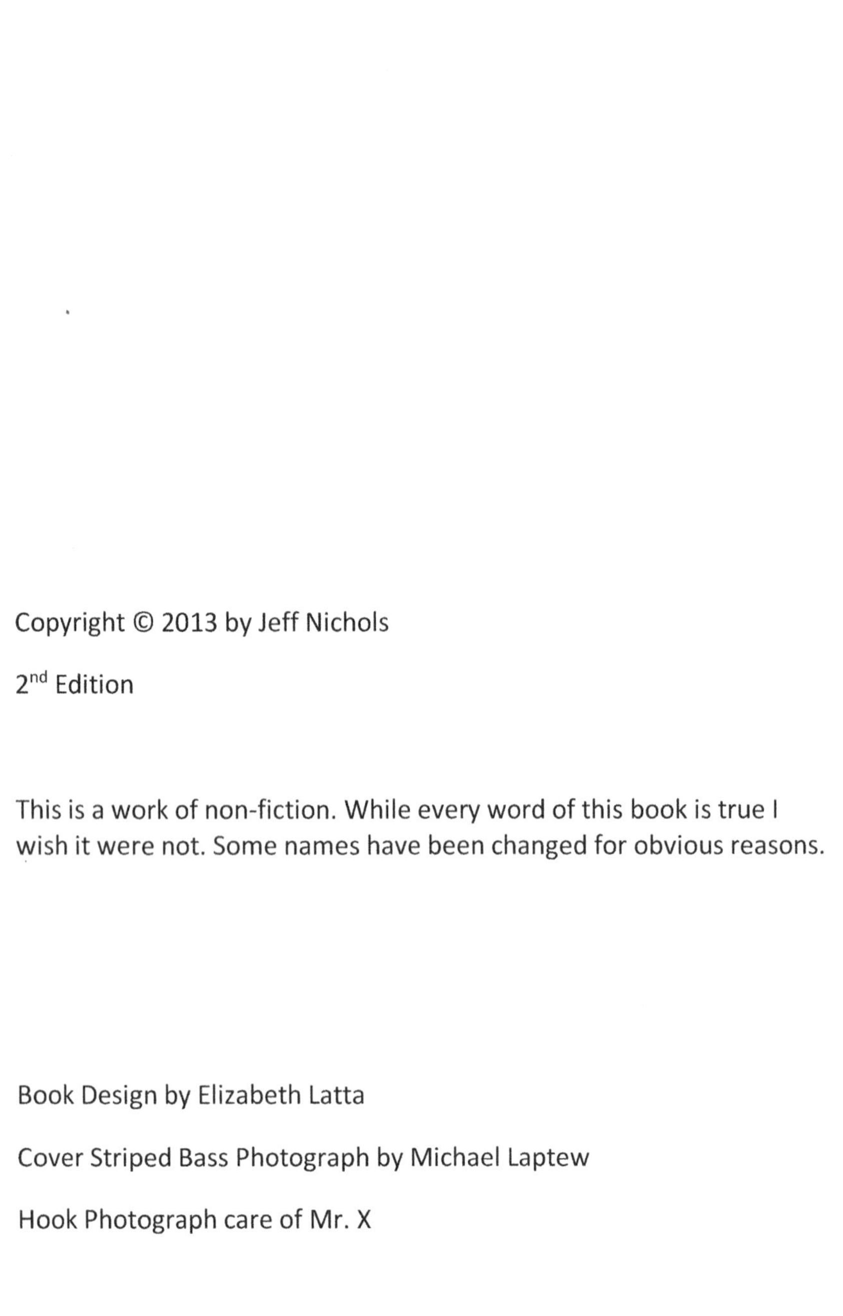

2nd Edition

This is a work of non-fiction. While every word of this book is true I wish it were not. Some names have been changed for obvious reasons.

Book Design by Elizabeth Latta

Cover Striped Bass Photograph by Michael Laptew

Hook Photograph care of Mr. X

Preface

Let us draw near with a true heart in full assurance of faith, with our hearts sprinkled clean from an evil conscience and our bodies washed with pure water.

Hebrews 10:22

I had mixed feelings about writing this book. Sure, I have always desired literary notoriety and am admittedly a media whore. But why would I want to piss off a Portuguese cook I used to sell fish to, or take the chance of provoking commercial fishermen? These fishermen are not far from becoming endangered species themselves, as a result of bad regulations created by government bureaucrats who are unacquainted with the realities of fishing. Or why alienate all my trophy fishing buddies?

I could have had another fun, inconspicuous, hassle-free season trophy hunting for big, female striped bass out on Block Island Sound -- The answer is I had to write this book because the "inconvenient truth" is that the striped bass, as inconceivable as it seems since they were so abundant only a few years ago, is in real trouble again, and may soon face complete collapse.

I have personally been on board a commercial dragger as a deck hand and was no mere witness; I was the unfortunate participant in the destruction of over three thousand pounds of striped bass which had come up in the nets and we were instructed to throw over the side dead. I felt obligated to document what I have seen, to give something back to a particular species of fish: the striped bass, the morone saxatilis, which has given me and many others so much joy over the years. People might say I'm courageous for writing this book, this may well have been the case if I had done so three years ago but now that the decline of the fishery is obvious lets hold off celebrating my efforts – hopefully it's not too late. It is almost as if I'm telling people not to drink the beer when the exhausted keg is making its final gasps.

I am aware that by writing this there was no way to avoid donning the hat of a hypocrite. Even if I had exhibited some discipline and stopped selling this fish out of the trunk of my car (as recently as last year), or had begun to throw back the big, female trophy-sized striped bass and let them live and spawn rather than bringing them back to the marina to weigh them in for ego's sake —perhaps then I would have the authority to take the pulpit and preach, but alas, this is not the case. Regrettably, I have to be that guy who says, "do what I say, not what I have done."

My hope is that this book will put a spotlight on an insidious practice which remains all too prevalent: the practice of illegally selling this fish to restaurants by recreational fishermen. While illegally selling one's catch to a restaurant may seem benign, compared to other illegal activities, it is hurting the legitimate licensed commercial fishermen that are trying to make an honest living by legitimately harvesting these fish by hook and line.

In the following pages, I also examine the black market that exists and is growing, in relation to these striped bass (also called rock fish). With regards to the notorious, illegally submerged gill net, found in the Chesapeake Bay by authorities in Maryland two years ago, a net containing close to ten tons of striped bass, I ask the following questions: where does such a massive amount of fish get shipped to?

How big is the criminal distribution network? Who is buying it? What name is it being sold and served under?

Hopefully I have illustrated how senseless and absurd it is to kill large female breeders and then bring them in for bragging rights at the dock. (I myself have done this countless times.) Finally, I have sought to expose the commercial draggers, with their massive destruction of resources and their undiscriminating nets.

"What has happened to the striped bass?" people ask, as they scratch their befuddled heads. The simple fact is that we killed them ... when only a few years ago, they had made a complete recovery and were in abundance up and down the East Coast. We killed them ... just like the American buffalo. We rounded them up in the name of commerce and ego. We killed them with nets, with spear guns and with rods and reels.

Greed and ego has once again depleted the striped bass biomass. Am I worried about pissing people off with this book? Yes! (I am paranoid and skittish to begin with.) However, the people that will be angry about this book are in all probability not acquainted with the history of the striped bass. They are unaware of a movement that took place over thirty years ago, which paved the way for the most abundant decade in striped bass history (2000-2010), abundant for both commercial and recreational fishermen alike. In the early eighties incredible sacrifices were made to save the striped bass from meeting the fate of the codfish. (As a result of over fishing by a fleet of international commercial net draggers in the 70's, the codfish has not, to this day, recovered as a sustainable fishery.) I am referring to the noble efforts of a remarkably small group of intensely dedicated individuals, individuals such as Rhode Island Captain Jim White, Dick Russell and his friends, Congresswoman Claudine Schneider and the late Republican Senator John H. Chaffee, who ultimately submitted a bill to protect this historic and important fish. The irony is that these people's lives were made very difficult (and in some cases actually threatened) by fishermen (recreational and commercial alike) who had no understanding of the basic concept of preservation, and yet benefited greatly (years later) from a moratorium that they were originally opposed to. The striped bass made an incredible comeback, and it had come perilously close to becoming extinct.

This season, for the sake of the morone saxatilis, why don't we put our two hundred dollar cell phones to use and just take a picture of the large female breeding fish and throw it back? I will. We are not living in 1938 when in order to document a trophy fish, you needed to kill it, drag it back to the marina, hoist the fish up on a scale, and call the local photographer who comes down and sets up a tripod, goes under that silly hood of his, and snaps his shot. Today we all walk around with cell phones capable of launching rockets. They have cameras in them that film producers only wish they had twenty years ago. Today there are very few taxidermists left to do skin mounts, so the only reason to keep a forty pound bass would be to eat it - and why do that if big fish are loaded with toxins? Take a picture and let her go as quickly as possible! Keep a smaller fish for the table...says he who weighed in just about every big fish he ever caught.

The real elephant in the room with regards to the striped bass world today is the bacterial disease mycobacteriosis, which has every bass fisherman, consciously or unconsciously, bummed out. It sucks. I wish I did not have to write about it; I am primarily a humorist and this is a brutal subject and a buzz kill. But no book on striped bass fishing worth its weight, can avoid this subject today. According to scientists, it originated in Chesapeake Bay which is the striped bass' primary breeding ground and is, unfortunately, highly polluted as a result of chemical run off of fertilizer and other chemicals and septic issues. It is said that up to seventy percent of the fish in the Chesapeake have this condition. The mysterious ailment characterized by red lesions is believed to be fatal to the fish. This fearful malady has gotten the attention of all striped bass fishermen even the most callous. It wears at our very soul and spirit. How could it not?

It is certainly a highly disturbing phenomenon, but there is no reason, at this point, to believe that mycobacteriosis is to the striped bass what phytophthora infestans was to the potato crops of Ireland years ago. Until more accurate assessments are done, there is no need to enter the realm of complete hysteria and despair regarding the fishery. Moreover, many fish don't have any marks on them at all, and not all fish with red marks and lesions have mycobacteriosis. Fish with the characteristic red marks and sores have been examined by both the Massachusetts Department of Marine Fisheries and the University of Virginia and have shown no traces of mycobacteriosis at all. History has shown that the striped bass is a tough and adaptive fish capable of spawning in many other areas than the contaminated Chesapeake Bay. They will ride out this blight. It is also encouraging that there appears to be more bunker (a small, oily-rich baitfish) around these days. Bunker is the striped bass' primary source of nutrition. This apparent, small resurgence of bunker should ultimately make the striped bass fishery stronger and healthier.

Okay, enough of the science stuff. I am now in a cold sweat; the two brain cells in my head are banging together so hard that smoke is coming out of my ears. (If I have to spell mycobacteriosis one more time my head may very well explode.) I am not a scientist; I am just a fishing addict with an ego problem. I happened to be armed with a captain's license I got by filling out a coupon I saw on the back of a Cracker Jack box. Yes, I took one of those crash, "get your captain's license in six weeks" courses; I admit it. When I first got my license in the mail, I literally did not know how to tie a boat to the dock, let alone back one up. On my first paid charter when the fog rolled in, I had to ask the customers if there was anyone on the boat acquainted with radar, and specifically how to turn one on. Luckily no one got hurt, and after ten years of taking people fishing, I guess I am worthy of the credential now. But let me make an appeal to the guys that got their captain's license the way I did: do everyone a favor, you silly gooses, and send your licenses back to where you got them. And no, I am not worried about losing charters over writing this stuff. I make no money as a charter boat captain after expenses. For me, a good charter is when the customers don't steal all my sinkers and take my rods. In my opinion, whoever wrote that book *Do What You Love and The Money Will Follow* should be beaten to within an inch of his life.

Anyway, unless you live in a cave, if you are a fisherman you know that the striped bass stocks are in trouble.

Some tough issues here for sure, but really, the majority of this book is a tale of one dope's fishing addiction (mine), that eventually leads him out to "Mecca", Montauk, New York, the self-anointed sport fishing capital of the world.

Acknowledgments

I am dyslexic and therefore a challenge to any editor. As my spelling is downright horrific; spell check is no match for me as it is not designed to deal with my phonetic ways. A few great editors volunteered to help me along the way: my father, Peter Nichols, and my friends Elizabeth Latta, and Daniel Rosengarten. I no doubt tried all of their patience, but they all came through for me. So thank you. I was in a hurry to get this book out for this coming striper season. I never tried to show it to a formal publisher. You may come across a typo or to (too? two?), but please believe me; we really tried to get them all. It is very hard, I have learned, to put together a coherent book. I also want to thank all my fishing pals both new and old who helped me with the facts.

Preface

Selling Fish to Feed an Addiction

As I sped back to Montauk Point, I saw that I was outrunning the Downeaster commercial fishing boat chasing me. The boat I was using wasn't mine. I had borrowed my friend's old twenty-two foot clunker, which did have a two-hundred horsepower outboard engine, but it didn't have great compression. I could only get twenty miles an hour out of her, but that was enough to get up on plane and run faster than the average Downeaster, which ran at fourteen knots wide open. I kept thinking *how could I put myself in this position again?* This was all I needed; a three hundred pound, crazed commercial fisherman and his posse of retired baymen- who looked like guys right out of the movie *Deliverance*- chasing me in this small boat, bellowing over the VHF radio that he was going to do bodily harm to me, knock my teeth in, etc.

I eventually turned the radio off so my horrified charter customers, huddled in the stern, did not have to hear the threats anymore. They were two striped bass enthusiasts from Maryland who were vacationing in Montauk I had loaded them onto this piece-of-crap boat that afternoon. They were to pay me five hundred bucks, which, by the way, is highly illegal, as my friend's boat was not a registered charter boat and was not insured as such. But that was the least of our problems now. I was just hoping that it would not break down. We could not use my own properly registered and insured twenty-four foot center console charter boat with the new Suzuki 225 four-stroke engine. Apparently my engine had been sabotaged and my boat was useless. My customers wanted to fish the Porgy Hump, a famous fishing spot about two and a half miles east of Montauk Point, for big striped bass and were unfortunate enough to click on my website, "Second Choice Charters," where I guaranteed a "40 Pound Bass. " (Striped bass over forty-pounds are also referred to as "pigs," "cows," and "slobs.")

I had, at one point a few years back, promised myself and my girlfriend that once I hit my goal of a fifty-pounder I would cut back on fishing. I now had three fifties under my belt and my addiction to catching huge striped bass seemed to be growing rather than waning. Worse, to pay for my addiction, I was now bringing unsuspecting and innocent people into harm's way.

Whenever the price of striped bass gets up to six dollars a pound tension always seems to mount between "bootleg", or black market fishermen, and legitimate licensed commercial fisherman. I had witnessed this scenario too many times, and I knew the threats this particular fisherman was making over the VHF were all too real. He was blind with rage. No one in Montauk wanted to deal with this particular guy. As a general rule you never want to tangle with anyone who makes a living with his hands; I would put a construction worker against a muscle bound gym rat any day. And this guy had worked for years stacking seventy-pound boxes of fish as if it was nothing for hours on end. Several times cops were called on him and a few captains had restraining orders against him.

But, in my favor, I also knew that I had a slightly faster boat than my enraged pursuer had and provided that he did not call ahead and have someone waiting for me at the dock (a very real chance), I would elude a beating this time around. I was already slightly paranoid walking around Montauk. I had a court case coming up and was being asked to testify against a certain commercial boat. Many were scared that I would rat on them.

I felt bad for the two guys who were with me. They had answered my ad, with its guarantee of landing a forty-pound striped bass. That was probably not going to happen. "Second Choice Charters" was now an overstatement. The big "cow" bass were out east on the Porgy Hump which was now quickly fading into the distance.

We had begun fishing in a spot just to the east of the Porgy Hump which has always held big bass. I had seen this particular commercial boat about a half-mile away, but we were so busy catching fish I did not see him sneak up on us, pull alongside us, and start screaming at me, accusing me of fishing on "his numbers," by which he meant coordinates of longitude and latitude. It was obvious by his rage that he believed I had sneaked on his boat, turned on his GPS and stolen his fishing spot. (While I was certainly capable of such a violation, in this case I was innocent.)

Even if I had done this, the Porgy Hump is the size of a football field. There was plenty of room for two boats. Back in the day there used to be fifty boats out there.

At first he calmly asked what I was doing there. I thought he meant what we were catching. I began to tell him that we were catching mostly small fish and were doing okay, and he interrupted me, his voice still very serious and calm but his stern facial expression betraying anger. "I meant, what are you doing on this spot?" I was now genuinely confused. I said something along the lines of, "What's so special about this spot?" and then, finally understanding what he was getting at, added, in as non-confrontational way as possible, that I had never even seen him fish this particular area. The commercial fisherman bridled at what he perceived as an apathetic response. His eyes rolled back like a shark and he unleashed a tirade of obscenities and what I knew to be very real threats. "If you did not have those people on your boat I would ram you right here...I will see *yous* at the marina," he snarled.

I did not want to mess with him, so I ate some crow. I apologized to my customers profusely. I was utterly mortified. I told the clients to reel up, and we headed to a place called Shagwong Rip that is only about a half-mile from Montauk Harbor. They looked shocked although they tried to appear nonchalant. I told the bewildered duo that the trip was not over; they would catch more fish, but we had to pick up and go back three miles to Shagwong Rip. As the money was up on the fish, I knew that the commercial guy would not leave a red-hot bite on the Porgy Hump until it got dark. It was around 7 pm in early August so we had at least an hour to fish. I told the customers that as soon as we saw that commercial boat break the horizon from the east coming from the Porgy Hump we had to scram back to the harbor ahead of them. I would pull up to the gas dock, they would unload their gear and fish and I would put the boat away as they got in their car. I told them it would take me five minutes, and that they should have their cars running. "You guys don't have to pay me, but that guy was serious, just get me out of Montauk to any train or bus station." They agreed to the terms.

We went to Shagwong Rip and they actually caught some more bass, and had steady action. But the air was tense; there was no laughing. Not much was said. Still in a state of shock, my anxiety was contagious and contaminated the mood of the trip. The entire time the customers were fishing I had my hand on the throttle and my eye glued to the east waiting to see that Downeaster show up over the horizon.

I was already on edge. At this very time I was being persuaded, with the threat of a possible six months imprisonment for violating Department of Environmental Conservation (D.E.C.) regulations, to testify against a certain dicey commercial fisherman I had worked for a few years back. People (captains, restaurant owners, and fish distributors) knowing the Machiavellian tactics the D.E.C. employed on people to extract information, were scared that I would talk. And like I said, my own personal boat had apparently been sabotaged. Things were not looking good.

From July to October selling striped bass illegally is a multi-million-dollar industry on Long Island, in Manhattan and the greater tri-state area. Rhode Island and Massachusetts are also well known for having robust black markets; many fish are illegally hustled through the backdoors of restaurants in these states. Most of the time the fish is presented on the menu as a special: "Fresh, Local Wild Striped Bass," and most of the time the fish were not purchased through legal channels, which is to say the owners of the restaurants bought the fish out of the trunk of some guy's car and not from a licensed fish market or fish distributor. Yes, the owners of the restaurant are taking a chance of being fined heavily or even shut down for accepting these undocumented fish. Still, no one wants to be the one restaurant in town that pays full wholesale prices. (At the time striped bass wholesale price was six bucks a pound for whole fish or twelve bucks a pound for the fillet.) On the black market it goes for as little at a dollar-fifty a pound for the whole fish and five to eight bucks a pound for fillets. Striped bass is an easy fish to prepare, cook and sell as a "wild, local fish". The average three to five-ounce filet can be sold as an entree for close to thirty-five bucks depending on the restaurant. A busy, high-end hundred-seat restaurant could bang out fifty striped bass specials a night.

Aside from depleting a valuable and, as many feel, sacred national resource, the real victims of this are the legitimate licensed commercial fisherman who have been authorized to harvest a prescribed amount of these fish by hook and line. When a guy like me sells my fish to restaurants to offset my fuel bill it drives the wholesale price down. This puts more pressure on the legitimate commercial guys who while trying to fish for a living are already feeling pressure from constricting regulations and skyrocketing operating expenses. These guys have become endangered species themselves.

There is another level of poaching striped bass where criminals use submerged gill nets to extract literally tons of striped bass a year. These fish are not sold to restaurants. The question as to where this half million ton or so of striped bass is trafficked to has authorities scratching their heads. One thing I am sure of: it is not being presented as striped bass (or "rockfish") on menus in Ohio. Is it being shipped overseas? Used for cat food, fertilizer? More on this later.

Striped bass have been incredibly abundant during the last decade as a result of catch limits and a federal moratorium on the species from the 1980's which allowed the fish to recover completely. In fact, some argue that at one point there may have been too many striped bass as they are apex predators that devour juvenile and mature lobsters, squid, fluke, flounder (and all their prey), and just about everything else that they can suck down that swims in their path.

These "fish people" knew that I was privy to a lot of information an outsider should not know. At the same time, I had made some strong bonds in Montauk - that sliver of a town on the eastern tip of Long Island - over the years, and most knew that I would not rat on anyone to avoid a fine.

Anyway, back to my story. We had been fishing for about thirty-five minutes or so when I saw over the horizon the distinctive bow of the Downeaster. I gave the command I was anxious to give: "Lines up!" and punched the throttle propelling the boat toward Montauk Harbor. I was a good two miles ahead of the Downeaster and I was going twenty-miles an hour. Although I'm not good at math, I knew that this would put us into the marina a good twenty minutes ahead of them. Of course, if he really was in a rage, he could push his Cummings diesel to 16 knots or even 17 knots - close to nineteen-miles an hour. That would make my window to put away the boat considerably shorter.

I was still confident that I could spray down the boat - if it had been my boat I would skip this part - then store the rods, tie the boat up, and get to the parking lot inside of ten minutes.

Putting the boat away took longer than I expected. As I was putting the last critical spring line on the boat (the line that keeps the boat from riding up onto the dock) the ominous commercial boat rounded the furthest bulkhead of the marina. He had his spotlight on, searching back and forth, near where my friend kept his boat. Since it was a full moon, I could not get the final spring rope on because the tide was so low.

It was like a horror movie where a girl gets her jacket caught on barbed wire or something just as Freddy Krueger is honing in on her. With one last flurry of energy brought on by shear adrenalin and maybe the last drop of testosterone I had left in my drug addled forty-five year old body, I was able to pull the rope over the cleat and secure the boat. As I ran, the spotlight found me and followed me right down the dock and into the back of the waiting truck. I screamed, "Go!" We drove west in silence for about two hours. They dropped me off at the Ronkonkoma train station, where I sat in deep thought, my legs shaking, on an empty platform waiting for over an hour for next train to Manhattan.

My story is not a new one. Back in the 1970's stories of ass-whippings were much more prevalent in Montauk and all fish docks across the northeast. When fishermen had no high-tech tools with which to find fish, no GPS, no radar, and no Loran, only the best at sighting landmarks could stay on "the meat." The only tools fishermen had were visual landmarks like buildings, buoys and lighthouses they could use to take "ranges" on important pieces of bottom. They would also use green fluorescent floating glow-sticks that they would attach to a line and sinker to mark where the large schools of strippers, the "money fish," were. The fishermen would see the glowing green stick just below the water line and know where to start their drift. Only a few boats were privy to these locations. The other boats were forced to bang it out in Pollock Rip, which was hit or miss. If you were invited in with these "pin hookers," you could make a lot of money selling fish. If you were not in the clique, you better find a new form of work. It once ended tragically. On July 8, 1975, a son of a well-known boat dealer, at the age of twenty-three, feeling ostracized by the fleet, entered Montauk Harbor, anchored his boat and blew his head off with a shotgun.

I say this not only to sensationalize, but also to illustrate that the selling of striped bass (a fish so popular in the northeast that mounts grace the walls in several courthouses and municipal buildings) can be serious business. It is said that if our nation had a fish rather than a bird as our national emblem it would be the striped bass.

Caught

Montauk in the Seventies was the closest New York State had to the Wild West. There were no Department of Conservation regulations on bass, so there was no real legal presence on the water aside from the Coast Guard - and because of high turnover of personnel, there weren't many experts on fisheries among them. (Why does it seem that three out of four people on the average Coast Guard boat seem to be young kids from Oklahoma?) At the docks and in the bars people handled things with their fists. People were not as litigious as they are today; they did not think of consequences. They did not have to. People simply either administered or took "a beating." I arrived in Montauk in 2002. I was not part of this ass-whipping era. I was white collar. I am a graduate of Hotchkiss tennis camp, I went to boarding school, I used to wear madras pants, and I skied in Vail. I have never delivered a beating and I wasn't certain if I could take one.

How did a kid who grew up on Park Avenue Manhattan and summered in the Cape and Nantucket get mixed up in the black market fish trade? Simple: I am a fishing addict. Not an addict like, "Ha, ha, he is a *fishaholic*!" but rather, "Holy shit, he lost his job, his wife, his children, his bank account, his friends, his life..." type of addict. It's real. I sold fish so I could fish more; one fed the other. There have been school teachers and postmen fired from their jobs for smelling like fish and coming in late (and it is very hard to get fired from the post office). Guys have refinanced their houses (back when they could) to pay for their boats and entry fees into tournaments. There has been bankruptcy, countless divorces and deaths, all in the pursuit of fish.

I began to sell striped bass to restaurants in Manhattan to pay for my addiction. So you say, "Yes, but fishing addiction is not as bad as heroin or crystal meth." Well maybe not as bad but arguably more destructive and expensive. when you factor in the expense of running a boat, the environmental impact (some fishing boats with old twin two-stroke engines kick-out more carbon emissions per hour than three hundred cars), the bait, the equipment...you get the picture. Not only that, but the truth of the matter is that the large (fourty-pound plus) striped bass, as they travel many times up polluted rivers like the Hudson to spawn, contain more toxic PCBs than the average fish. Some scientists believe it's not healthy to eat more than a couple of servings a month. And I peddled this stuff to restaurants for years! Seriously, in a way the crystal meth addict is less destructive than a fishing addict. Think about it. A meth-head tinkers with stuff; a meth-head will find an old radio in a dumpster and fix it. How harmful is that? Sure, his teeth and hair will fall out shortly, but I have made my point, I guess.

In this book I speak of "pin hookers." They are a group of commercial fisherman who are licensed by the state to catch certain fish with a rod and reel and sell them. Many used to be haul seine netters, who hauled in fish to the beach with a net. When the government outlawed, for good reason, the industrial netting of striped bass off the Long Island beaches the haul seiners were awarded compensation and given permission to catch a certain quota of bass a year from a boat using rod and reel. I interacted with some of these guys over the years and for the most part they are decent, hard-working people, but that one particular Pin Hooker did *not* like me.

The train finally came and I went back to my empty apartment in on Park Avenue. When I say empty, I mean empty not only of people but things. No rug or lamps; just a chair and a small couch. The note my ex-girlfriend left me months before basically telling me: fuck you, you chose fishing over me, still sat on the kitchen counter. Everything was gone, even the coffee maker. Wire cables hung down from the wall where my girlfriend's flat-screen TV used to rest. My memories of this place went past my girlfriend. I was once a baby in arms in this large three-bedroom apartment overlooking the opulent boulevard. There must have been such promise for me then, as my grandfather was a captain of industry who ran a large wool company in the northeast. Both my grandfather and father attended Ivy League colleges and went on to do good things. Now, decades later, I sat in the living room in the only chair left, reeking of fish.

After sitting for a minute I got up and went over to my neighbor's apartment, an eighty-five-year-old WWII vet. He wasn't the nicest of men and drank heavily, but we had a working relationship. When I was in town, I would go to the bank for him and run small errands, and take out garbage etc. I would sit and talk with him. Smart man. Anyway, about five years before he had asked me to sign some paperwork. It was a form stating that if he died, I would return his gun to the local police precinct. (I guess this is protocol.)

I had a key to his apartment. I knew he would not hear the bell and he could not get around all that well. He basically sat in his back room and watched movies on his computer and drank. I opened the door to the apartment, went to the back, to his bedroom and knocked on the door. Sure enough, he was sitting in front of his computer watching a movie. He was happy enough to see me. "I'm fine," I said, "but I need to borrow your gun." He looked up at me, studying me: "You're not going to eat the barrel, are you?" I said no. I just needed it for protection that night and that I would return it. I went back into my apartment, put the gun case down on the table, opened it and took out the gun pieces. I then assembled the gun putting the cartridge in as he had showed me years before. I was blind with anger. I had many options. I could sit there and wait or be proactive. I could strike first. If I was going to "eat the barrel," like my old neighbor feared, I had a few people I was going to take down before I met that fate, and one was that greasy commercial fisherman.

Funny, as I write this it sounds so melodramatic, but that is exactly how I felt at the time. I wanted to strike before I was struck... I had no kids, no girlfriend, no money, and no career to speak of. As the saying goes in prison: *don't fuck with broke and crazy!* I sat there for about an hour, genuinely frightened for my life and completely disillusioned with Montauk and the larger fishing industry in general. My honeymoon with Montauk was over. Montauk really was a "quiet little drinking village with a fishing problem..." as the cheeky and apt little phrase goes. Montauk, a place that once provided me with immense happiness, had come to represent greed, abuse, and egos gone wild.

*

How It Started

My first memories of fishing are wholesome and wonderful. They start when I was around eight or nine, maybe ten. In the early 70's my sister, my mother, father and I would make the pilgrimage up I-95 from New York City and down to my Grandfather's enchanted summer home in Harwichport, Cape Cod. It was a sprawling compound of a house overlooking Nantucket Sound, an old house, probably built in the late 17th century. We descended on the house for two weeks every August. My poor overwhelmed grandparents sought refuge in their small apartment above the garage, Anne Frank style. It was rumored that behind one of the fireplaces in the main house was a hiding place where slaves hid during the Civil War. My always-curious mother simply had to see if this was true, and to me and my sister's delights (not so much my grandparents'), knocked down part of the fireplace. Low and behold there was a little room back there.

As big as the house was with its expansive three sections, it was eventually sold and moved down the road. In its place now stands a much bigger house. It is impressive but sadly a bit plain and ordinary and well... just too big.

While other kids hung out at the Wychmere Harbor Yacht Club participating in regattas and sailing school, I was drawn, to the disapproval of my grandfather, by an unseen hand down to the public docks in town where I would show up at three in the afternoon to watch the charter fishing boats come in from fishing off the south side of Nantucket, "the shoals." Now granted, at that young age, as we all know, everything appears *cool* and *amazing*. But to me, watching the happy customers scramble off the small Downeaster charter boats and watching the captains or mates unload fish after fish from huge boxes onto the docks, so spectators could ooh and ah over a nice mixture of big bass and blues, was nothing less than truly mesmerizing. There were no limits in the early 70's; the more fish the better. The idea of fish conservation, let alone the practice of it, would not be established for another ten years or so. The customers would take what they wanted and then fishermen would pull up in their Ford pick-up trucks and fill the back with fish. They would drive off to sell them. Because there was no ice they couldn't have been going far; maybe Thompson's clam bar at the end of the street. It seemed like such a normal and guilt-free activity, all so simple and natural. Who would think that in the years to come selling fish directly to restaurants would be illegal, causing a huge black market fishing industry to emerge, and fishermen to be labeled criminals?

Jeff Nichols

I loved the smell of the docks: a mix of motor oil, diesel fuel, bleach and rotting fish. Our senses are so alive when we are young. Everything was thrilling at that age. Even a simple drive to a destination, or knowing it was Friday, was earth shaking; wasn't it? I remember an old girlfriend telling me once that when she was a young girl she had to share space with her sisters. Once one moved out she was thrilled - actually thrilled - to have her own drawer to put stuff in! And to think, thirty years later and we are all guzzling down our Prozac with black coffee just to try and approximate a smile. Fishing for me – the concept, the mystery, the equipment, the tough looking captains, the *industry* of it all – was like the first time I was exposed to rock music-groups like *Kansas*, *Boston*, and *Tull*. It absolutely blew my mind. I think I fell in love with Montauk as an adult because it had that same smell as Wychmere Harbor. Maybe that smell I referred to, boat soap mixed with decomposing baitfish baking on the hot wooden docks, sounds like an odd thing to derive pleasure from, but I loved it and still do. It's analogous, perhaps, to the alcoholic's loving the smell of a gin mill - which is not as exciting for most people.

I remember that all around the periphery of the parking at the docks there were little wooden fish shacks. Some of them were completely dilapidated with broken windows. I think those used to belong to the commercial guys because I remember huge nets, flags and orange buoys inside, all tools of the trade, when I peeked in the windows in utter awe. I visited Harwichport a few years back with my dog Columbo. The docks themselves had less character and seemed fairly sterile - they got rid of the wooden docks and commercial boats (where were the lobstermen?) And they just had one cement pier. But to my happiness the shacks or fishing huts are still there now! With nets in them!

Caught

One captain was particularly nice to me at the docks, Captain Bob, owner of the boat called the OJ. It was a small Downeaster lobster boat, between thirty and forty feet. I guess at one point I must have asked him if I could tag along one day. He must have said if it was all right with the customers and all right with my mom I could go. So my adventurous mom threw caution to the wind and brought me to the docks at 6 am. Captain Bob ran the idea by the charter, two nice couples, as planned. They gave me the green light, and we were off.

It was a long ride to Monomoy Point and around Nantucket Island to the shoals where we were to fish. I looked at a map recently and it is probably over thirty miles one way. For those slow Downeaster boats it must have taken two hours just to get there. Perhaps, if my first visit to these fishing grounds off this storied island had been on a nice clear day, my memory of the trip would not be so spectacularly vivid. It was foggy, *pea soup*, when we got to the fishing area; we could not see but we could hear seagulls and gannets diving and singing, trying to catch the baitfish jumping out of the water in their desperate effort to avoid being eaten by the bigger fish that preyed upon them. This was the very definition of wild. This was the food chain at work, big prey after little prey...and we were in the thick of this phenomenon. It is still like this on our waters today, a tremendous sight. May we never lose this.

I remember the lures Captain Bob used. One was called a Hoochy Troll and consisted of a plastic skirt, pulled over what looked like a ball bearing chain. The Hoochy Troll had a single hook on the end of it. He used different colors: green, red, orange, rainbow, black- depending what was working best. He had many of these lures. They came in nice white boxes. I remember being impressed by the clean, white-wax covered, little cardboard boxes that were stacked neatly and were filled with the Hoochy Troll lures. This was very much a professional operation I was associated with.

As we let out the line, we would occasionally see another charter boat come through, then just as quickly, vanish back into the fog. I guess the captains where communicating by VHF radio, and maybe they had some type of locating system. How did they know where they were? I guess they were all lining up to fish a rip, trying to make the same pass. Then the fish started to come over the side, one after another. I watched these men and women wrestle these fish, quietly encouraging one another - a few blues and then a big striper. Then it was my turn; how could they not let the renegade stowaway take a crack at it? I remember I had a fish close to the boat when the hook pulled out at the last minute. I watched helplessly as the bass drifted back under the surface. I did not catch this fish that day. Perhaps this failure, "the one that got away," stayed with me and worked on my subconscious, eventually creating an impulse to slaughter every fish I came across for decades to come.

Though I hated to leave Cape Cod at the end of our two-week summer vacation, I was lucky to be able to return to another fishing paradise. My parents had a country home just fifty miles north of Manhattan that was perched on an idyllic spring fed lake/pond in the Sedgewood Club, Carmel, NY.

I am not sure what distinguishes a pond from a lake, but it can't just be size because China Lake is small. It's maybe three hundred yards long and two hundred yards wide at best, but deep. Parts of China Lake hit sixty feet. When we swam near the bottom we could actually feel the spring coming from the lake's floor, cold and strong. There were very few houses on the lake at the time, maybe nine as opposed to fifteen now. They were modest little cottages. None of them had big lawns and since they were primarily weekend places, septic problems were not yet an issue. In fact, we drank the water unfiltered. The conditions were conducive to supporting a healthy ecosystem. And a robust ecosystem it was. Sit a minute at the edge of China Lake in the 70's or 80's and you would basically see an aquarium swim by, schools of yellow perch, their cousin white perch, various sized sun fish and crappies and then the minnows also called shiners and saw bellies. Hundreds of scared quick-moving minnows grouped together to look bigger. And then, of course on cue, the minnows' nemesis confidently moseys by, a big old largemouth or smallmouth bass. You could not see the pickerel because they were hiding in the grass, or the catfish, because they stayed in deeper water.

In the sandy areas of China Lake all one had to do was put a foot in the water to make twenty crayfish lunge backward with their tails in the air and resettle away from you in a confrontational pose, their claws up to try to frighten you as if saying "Okay, bring it on!" As kids we all loved to get plastic cups and try and catch these marvelously spunky little lobsters. There was also the occasional visit by a water snake, which sent all swimmers frantically swimming to the dock as if it was a ravenous great white shark looking for lunch. For days no one would go in the water after sighting a benign water snake. At night we would go to bed with bullfrogs roaring, and crickets singing and thunderous splashing, presumably trout rounding up the baitfish.

The fishing was great. The pond was stocked every year with trout: brook, rainbow, golden and brown. Just as we did in the charter boats off the Cape, we would troll for them. My dad and I would take our small aluminum rowboat (which occasionally leaked) and slowly move around the periphery of the lake. We constantly altered the speed of the boat to make the lure, either a Phipps "Feebee" or a Flatfish or a

Rooster Tail, appealing to our prey. We also tried to place the lure in the water column where the fish were. I am sure a lot of it was blind luck. We had no fish finder or electronics of any kind. When we did it right we'd get the "wack." We had no rod holders so the light rod would go shooting off. Sometimes we would barely grab it in time with our feet before it had a chance to shoot off the side of the boat. One thing is for sure, I did not have ADD, which I was later diagnosed with, when I was rowing around that lake, eyes glued to the tip of the rod waiting for the strike. In fact I was hyper focused.

When winter came it was time for ice fishing with my old friend Judge Dickinson, a Putnam County Supreme Court Justice. Sometimes the pond froze over by Christmas time. It happened quickly if there was freezing temperatures coupled with no wind. The next day a sheet of clear black ice would cover the entire lake. All you needed was an inch and a half to walk on, five inches to drive a truck across. You knew it was hard when it cracked and rumbled and moaned like a whale.

While others occasionally fished on the lake Judge Dickinson, "the Judge," wore a distinctive orange hunting jacket. I would awake around 7 am to the sound of drilling, look out my window and peer through the trees trying to get a glimpse of that orange jacket. Once I saw the orange jacket I would rejoice. I would bolt out of the house, my mother chasing me with a mitten or a hat or even a boot that I forgot. I was a learning disabled young boy. I was always very sloppy and had a tough time in sports and at school, but something about fishing- the gear, the camaraderie, the patience, the anticipation and the thrill of the reward, the possibility of a trophy fish, all appealed to me.

I would run across the ice, watching out for soft spots, and assist the Judge with skimming out the holes after he drilled them with his power Eskimo auger. Then we would set out the tip-ups; we were allowed five each by law. It was a very simple concept: three thin pieces of wood connected by a bolt with a spool of line at the bottom and a piece of metal sticking out. If a fish took the line, it tripped a thin metal wire and made an orange flag pop up to indicate that a fish was on. This would happen five to ten times on a good day, none on a bad day. I would be sitting there talking to the Judge, as he drank his homemade cider, and frying up some venison that he hunted in the fall. The conversation was always about fishing: his old friend Elmer's eight-pound chain pickerel, his grandson's ten- pound lake trout that he caught on Gleneida Lake in Carmel, and so on. It was always about big fish.

The Judge liked me - how could he not like a kid that into fishing? – But he also liked having someone to talk to. Then a flag would pop up indicating a fish had hit one of our lines! (Sometimes on a crisp day you could hear it snap before you saw it.) I would run over. Sometimes the entire tip-up would be shaking with a big fish. Sometimes the line would be screaming out - that usually meant a smallmouth or largemouth bass. Other times the line would be just sitting there out to one side or another - that meant a pickerel. Mostly we caught chain and grass pickerel and yellow perch. The Judge would make pickerel fish sticks and pickerel salad out of those, but occasionally we would get a nice trout.

One day, I was out picking up our lines to go home and as I began to pull the line in I was met with resistance. Something big and alive was on the end of the line. For some reason the flag had not popped up; it may have been frozen. I started to pull, trembling with anticipation. The scary giant hooked-jawed brown trout that appeared at the hole was more than I could handle. It had a huge eye that stared back at me. I screamed and the Judge came running over. I gave the line to him and he craftily negotiated the giant fish through the small hole. God, did we rejoice. The trout weighed six and a half pounds. My father got it mounted for me and it proudly hung on the mantelpiece adorning the living room for many years before a tragic fire took it. This was it for me; from here on out I associated catching big trophy fish with unmitigated pride and pleasure.

Then like every boy I hit puberty and from thirteen to twenty-two, or so, it was all about girls and partying with friends. I did keep fishing, but it was no longer my primary source of pleasure. On weekends I would return home from boarding school and bass fish at dusk for nice sized largemouth bass in neighboring Barret Pond. That was great fun. But I was also busy trying to get into college; this was not easy for a dyslexic who got 480 on his SATs. (Yes, that was a combined score.)

I got into Hobart in upstate Geneva, New York. At college, as with most of us, my drinking really took off. I was a liberal arts major which basically meant I could do whatever I wanted for four years, and had unlimited free time. Fishing was way down the list of things to do. Ahead of fishing were fraternity parties, girls, drugs and Grateful Dead shows. Although I was not a natural athlete or a jock, when that alcohol hit my system I felt strong, attractive, loose and athletic. National Lampoon's *Animal House* had just come out and fat, drunk and stupid was certainly in. Being a party animal became my identity. I was very popular at my college. Yes, we drank too much, but there were great people at Hobart; I liked everyone. I drank massive amounts of cheap keg beer often supplemented with drugs. Although I hated the feeling of dislocation, I smoked pot virtually every day. Even with all these distractions I found time to fish. Even in my oblivion, I could not help but notice that Hobart rested on the northwest corner of majestic

Seneca Lake. (Also a glacier lake known to be hundreds of feet deep.) And I did fish it.

I had some great friends who were like-minded. We rented a small boat one day in March and landed a nice 17-pound northern pike. One of my fraternity brothers knew a lot about lake trout fishing and he was all set up with the boat and gear. He taught me a lot about patience and finding the right temperature zones where the trout could be. On one trip we put in six hours to raise one trout and we were very happy with that. (Funny; today, if we don't catch 10 big striped bass, at least one over forty pounds, in one trip we are disappointed.) We also chartered a boat up on Lake Ontario, where they trolled for lake trout with downriggers. I loved to cast for pike off the jetties, but I probably only did this five times in four years. By the way, when I was on cocaine I never wanted to fish. I wanted to talk about it a lot - like an idiot, cooped up in a room, but the "dummy dust" made me afraid of the outdoors. Not so with acid. On acid I had to be outside appreciating nature's splendor. But I was NOT good at picking up girls when I was on acid. I do NOT recommend this (or acid). Anyway, I digress....

Still, fishing was always in my blood. If I and a bunch of college friends were at a beach somewhere on Long Island and we saw birds circling on the water (usually indicating that there was a school of bluefish chasing bait) and they came remotely near the beach (there were no stripers in '87), I would grab a surf rod and that would be it. I would follow that school of fish and birds until either I lost my lure or they swam out too far from shore, out of casting range. Even then I would sit down on the beach and wait in case they came back. It was still in my blood. I needed to get a boat!

I had been to Montauk only once during college. In 1989 we happened to charter the Blue Fin Four with Captain Michael Potts, a fishing legend in the area, a second-generation charter boat captain. We got our fair share of bluefish and the captain was amazed with my stepbrother, Mike, a smart guy and good angler who also had a sensitive side. He did not have the "Kill 'em all Big and Small" attitude I had. I remember Mike pushing down the sharp barbs on the hooks on a Holapopper when we caught bass in China Lake. I asked him why he was doing that, and he said, "Just to give the fish a little more of a chance." I remember being baffled by this.

We also once landed a five-pound brown trout while in a leaky rowboat full of water in April. The water temp was probably fifty degrees and we were probably 100 yards away from shore. God, we could have drowned so easily.

Anyway, Potts was surprised when Mike landed a keeper striped bass. Probably eighteen pounds or so; back then they had to be thirty-four inches. Mike's bass was a relatively big deal at the time when stripers were just starting to rebound after coming back from the brink of extinction and the moratorium. Just ten years later a charter boat like this would get his limit of twelve bass between fifteen and twenty-five pounds in two hours of fishing, then start to throw them back or head on to target another species.

I put a trip together in 1990. Montauk was always the ultimate destination, the self-proclaimed sport fishing capital of the world and I had heard that they were catching yellowfin tuna by the trashcan full just fifteen miles off shore at a place called the Butter Fish Hole. There was no internet then so I called the Chamber of Commerce and requested brochures on all the charter boats. I was so excited when they showed up in the mail. I looked at every pamphlet carefully reading the captain's credentials and bio and scrutinizing the quality of the boat. (Now after fifteen years of bass fishing, I realize that the boat is really not that important. The boat is merely a platform to catch fish. You want a boat that floats, working equipment and a fun captain and, most importantly, the fish have to be there. No matter how nice the boat if the fish aren't there it sucks.) Then I went to work marshalling the crew— a group of guys I thought everyone would get along with. As anyone who has done this can tell you, getting six guys together on one particular day, and getting them to cough up one hundred and twenty five bucks each was no easy feat, but I managed.

The trip, as it turned out, was a flop. We were subjected to the old bait and switch. The captain told us his boat was broken and took us out on a much smaller boat. We did not go for yellows but tried to get a giant ten miles off. We only used one rod and I don't think we even chummed (to attract the fish). I may be entirely wrong, but looking back I believe the guy phoned it in. As a captain I never did this. In Montauk something is always biting somewhere; coming home without fish was never an option on my boat. I am not bragging, just saying how it was. We ended up with one bluefish that day. Despite the bad trip and the lackluster captain, on the way in I asked him when his boat would be fixed and he told me that it would be running for a trip tomorrow. Tomorrow! This guy got to go out fishing again...tomorrow!! To me this was mind blowing. As we all scurried back to Manhattan to work Monday at our various jobs (I was probably telemarketing, or selling photocopy machines) what that captain said resonated with me. To me being a charter boat captain had to be the greatest job in the world by far! "What do I do for a living?" "...Well... I fish. What do you do?" "Oh you are a corporate lawyer. I'm sorry to hear that!"

I did not pursue my interest in charter fishing at the time; if I had I might have made a go at it. The 1990's were a great time because Montauk road traffic was light driving out there on route 27. It had not yet been choked off by the “trade parade” caused by the absurd building boom of 2000, where everyone took out mortgages, recklessly given out by banks, to build guesthouses, add new kitchens, and put in new bathrooms. Despite phenomenal fishing in Montauk from 2002-2010 fisherman could not make it through the pile-up of construction trucks at the point where route 27 turns into a single lane.

In the 1990’s there were not many government restrictions so people could catch and keep fish. Asians and Russians used to flock out there by the busload - and the tuna, everyone wanted the yellowfin when they were close. But I went on to pursue more traditional careers. All of which were more or less flops... including ten years as a stand-up comic. To assume that I could make it as a charter fishing captain is a big assumption... a busy charter boat captain has to be not only good with customers but very handy, organized and efficient. I sadly have always been a chronic slob and remarkably un- handy.

Really, when I think about it, being shot out of a cannon at the county fair would have been the perfect job for me, ideal for the person who craves fame but has limited job skills and talent. I mean when that guy is waving to the crowd before he gets hurled across a parking lot or cornfield, all eyes are on him; at that moment in time he is the man. I looked into it...there are very few jobs left in this once robust industry.

I have always wanted to be famous. In high school I wanted to be a jock. I made the lacrosse team only because I went to a small special education boarding school in Connecticut. There were a few good players on the team, but rather than pass them the ball I would shoot. The worst thing that happened to me was that I scored a goal on my second or third attempt. It gave me an exaggerated sense of my own abilities. That season I had like a hundred shots and three goals. Of course, I just remember the three goals. In hindsight, they were anemic shots that were so soft they must have thrown the unsuspecting goalie off. "Really, that's a shot? You have got to be kidding me," he may have thought to himself as the ball trickled by him. After graduating Hobart College for years I used to tell people that I played a season of B-team lacrosse at Hobart College, a division one powerhouse. Finally, one day I stopped doing this, as I realized I was just lying to myself. While I was a fast and strong little pecker...I did not have the stick skills or field awareness to play Division 1.

Being a stand-up comic was fun, exciting and terrifying. The only high that comes close to landing a big fish is getting your material to work in front of a group of strangers. You are floating after the show and it lasts through the next day. For the most part audiences were great to me. My material was very self-deprecating. My idol was Rodney Dangerfield. He is still my favorite; he pulled off the self-deprecating act better than anyone. I just did not have that wonderful accessible persona that Dangerfield had. But once in a while I would kill and got a little taste of what fame would be like; I pursued this feeling the same way I would later pursue a sixty-pound striped bass.

I traveled all over the country and opened for some big names like Comedy Central's Lewis Black and Robert Kline. In New York as an MC at Stand Up NY comedy club I would bring up the likes of Robin Williams and Chris Rock when they stopped by to work on their acts. Though other comics liked me, and the audiences were great to me- I was never that comfortable on stage. I also got into trouble - just like in college; I cheated. On the road you are asked to do a half hour of material, sometimes forty-five minutes. I had at best thirteen minutes of good stuff and I could work the crowd for another ten minutes, but still I needed to fill another ten minutes. So I stole jokes. Most of them were stock, "Two men walk into a bar with a parrot and a zebra" type jokes with real hack lines, but some, a couple, were blatantly lifted from other comics' acts. My distorted sense of entitlement, the same entitlement that would later allow me to illegally sell fish, was at full bore. It was sad really because the crowd is so pedestrian at these clubs, sometimes hack-y stuff works best. My jokes were clever, not hit them in the gut funny. It takes real discipline to stay true to your act. The reality was, if I did not have enough of my own material, and was not able to stay committed to it even if it meant bombing, I should not have been a professional comic. At that time, I just wanted to be famous so I could get women. Eventually I was caught and driven out of that business like Frankenstein being chased out of town by an angry mob with torches and pitchforks.

*

Striped Bass were Always on My Mind; The River Rats

While I could not get a proper career off the ground I was always attracted to striped bass fishing. When the *NY Post* ran an article in the early 90's about a group of mostly Latinos, who called themselves the "river rats," who were lining the East River and pulling in the occasional twenty-five pound striper, a huge fish for that time, I had to get in on this action. I was living In Sunnyside Queens then. I bought a rather cheap surfcasting pole and some clams from an outfit on Northern Boulevard, took a subway into Manhattan with the huge phone pole of a rod in hand, and went up to the East River between 100th and 120th streets in Spanish Harlem. Sure enough, there were around fifteen to twenty fishermen, all Hispanic, and all dutifully staring at the ends of their rods, most of which had bells on them to indicate when a fish hit. Some guys had as many as three rods out.

It was one of those very warm Junes. I remember baking in the sun with the sound of cars whipping buy on the FDR expressway, blowing out exhaust just feet from where we were fishing. I did see a few guys catch some nice bass (nothing over thirty pounds), but they were able to cast their bunker chunks (bait) way out, well near fifty yards, to a deeper channel. Striped bass don't generally swim along the shore of the East River, unless they become lost in pursuit of a huge school of bait. Rather, they pass by in the deeper channels. I can't remember why I could not cast far enough to hit the channel – perhaps it was a combination of the cheap pole, bad casting technique, too much or too little weight, too heavy a line, too light a line, who knows – but I simply could not cast far enough out. I spent probably three days walking up and down that river in the baking sun trying to catch a bass on a clam chunk. Finally, directly under the Triborough Bridge (now the Robert Kennedy), I hooked, landed and released a twenty-six inch striper. I was thrilled and fished another two days without a bite. I am sure I never used sun block, which is why my skin now looks like I live two miles from the sun.

Before I quit comedy I was able to get a manuscript I wrote to an agent in Hollywood. It was mostly about me growing up as a special education student and all the jobs I screwed up in the work place. The book was not great, but one of the chapters described a brief stint I had working on a commercial dragger off Long Island. It was a horrible experience, where I witnessed the senseless massacre and waste of thousands of pounds of beautiful fish. Subsequently the first thing I ever had published was a hundred and fifty thousand-word letter to the editor about this experience in *The Fisherman* magazine where it was printed, typos and all, on the inside cover. I simply had to document what I saw, which I did in this book. Anyway, a major production company behind movies like *Eternal Sunshine of the Spotless Mind, 21 Grams*, and Academy Award winner *In the Bedroom* was interested in making my book manuscript into a movie (which they eventually did: *American Loser,* released on DVD by Lionsgate Films in 2011). I received ten thousand dollars in option money. Now I could buy a boat!

It was now the mid-90s and the striped bass were on the comeback. Not knowing a thing about boats, I immediately went out and plopped down five-grand on the first craft I saw, an unimpressive old twenty-one foot Bayliner. I kept it at my friend's marina near Moriches Inlet on Long Island. It was fine for the bay but woefully inadequate for the punishing Moriches and ocean beyond.

Instead of using this boat I teamed up with my stepbrother's cousin from Mastic-Shirley. 'Cousin' Kenny (not my real cousin) had a seaworthy twenty-five foot Grady White. Though it was always breaking down, Kenny was mechanically inclined and always seemed able to eventually, somehow, come up with this part or that, to get things running again. Cousin Kenny was a tough son-of-a-bitch. Kenny was no little rich boy like me. Kenny did not attend boarding school, summer on Cape Cod or at Hotchkiss tennis camp. If anyone is familiar with Mastic-Shirley, Long Island you will know what I am talking about. It is hard to believe that it is even part of Long Island. I am not going to say that Mastic-Shirley is a high crime area, but I am pretty sure they filmed an episode of the show *Cops* there once.

But the love of fishing transcends all social and economic barriers. Kenny loved to fish as much as I did and we became fast friends. We would recklessly drive his boat out of the dangerous Moriches Inlet over to a sandbar with ten foot waves crashing over it. (More people have drowned while fishing Moriches Inlet than Montauk in the last few decades.) We cast our lures into the white water where disoriented baitfish tried to recover after being smashed by a breaking wave. There in the suds bass would prey on them. We used surface plugs and on many days easily caught one bass after another, all between twelve and eighteen pounds, I would say. I don't remember if we even kept one fish; it was all catch and release. Two fools out on the ocean having fun fishing. One of us would drive the boat, keeping the bow into the waves and be ready, if need be, to punch up a braking wave, which happened often, while the other would fish. We had a blast. I am sure that learning how to drive a boat in these hazardous conditions allowed me in later years to pull through some pretty harrowing conditions in Montauk.

Kenny was indeed a tad crazy. One time he took me shark fishing and we landed what was clearly a blue shark. Though the fish had none of the definable characteristics of an edible mako shark (symmetrical tail, mouth dense with sharp teeth, vicious), and all of the characteristics of a blue shark (no real teeth to speak of, long and skinny, docile), Cousin Kenny insisted that it was a mako. He ended up bringing the shark back to the dock, cutting the fish up (a blue shark has no bladder and pees though its skin, making the meat taste horrible) and had me pass out bags of rancid fillets to his neighbors as a friendly gesture. I could not look them in the eye as I handed them the bag and told them it was from Cousin Kenny. Some looked appropriately skeptical but took the offer anyway. Kenny also, somehow, sold a large section of the blue shark to a restaurant in Shirley for twenty-five dollars. That poor guy who bought the inedible shark must have gotten some bad feedback. On a related note, one of the reasons why one should not order swordfish from a menu is that often times it is really thresher shark or mako; they both present the same way (heart shaped/dark skin/white meat) as a swordfish filet will on a plate.

While fishing was good in Moriches we always talked about Montauk like it was a sacred place. "Mecca," as everyone referred to it. Finally, when we got a good break in the weather we drove via ocean the fifty miles out to Montauk to spend the week fishing. It was a nice trip; it is the only way to get a real glimpse of the waterfront mansions of the Hamptons. By car large hedges block the view but from the water you see these huge places dead on, from Seinfield's enormous house in South Hampton right down to Paul Simon's in Montauk and also the late Andy Warhol's little yellow cottages. I did this trip once in the middle of July at around 9 pm on a Saturday and was surprised to see that a lot of the homes looked vacant, not one light on! Probably owned by Europeans or banks, I guess.

When Kenny and I first rounded Montauk, "the point," we saw birds working and I launched a pencil popper right into the middle of the school. I hooked up right away. It was an amazing fight; the best pound for pound I may have ever had from any fish. It turned out to be an eight-pound little tunny (referred to locally as false albacore), or "albie," which I had side hooked. I was thrilled; I had never caught one before. When we pulled into the docks I walked around the marina proudly. We were in the sport fishing fish capital of the world, a place that does not bat an eyelid at the sight of a two hundred pound tuna, and I thought I was the man for landing this eight-pound albie. The next trip we were not so lucky.

Our plan was to go out to eel fishing at night for bass. That is when people were getting the slobs. The year was '97 so striper fishing was still far away from its peak in 2006, but boats were getting some nice fish in the thirty to thirty-five pound range. We did not get a hit. I think we were using too much weight. Kenny insisted I let my sinker stay right on the bottom and as a result my sinker was constantly getting snagged. It ended in the loss of the rig. If only not catching fish was the worst thing that happened to us that night.

Toward around one am the fog rolled in and the wind picked up. Though they were now being widely used by most boats, we had no GPS, radar or Loran. Kenny instructed me to go sit on the bow and look for rocks and boats and listen and point in the direction where the lighthouse horn was coming from. There was so much fog we could not see the lighthouse beacon. I don't know why Kenny was having such problems. Today I could make it home from the point going on a heading of 270 west. He must not have known this. In heavy seas it is tough to get a compass heading I must admit. The compass just starts spinning like the head of the child in *The Exorcist*. For at least an hour Kenny spun the boat around trying to find a heading on the compass. He would start out ok then yell, "Shit!" and start all over again yelling at me to point to the lighthouse.

This, pointing to the lighthouse where the foghorn was coming from, might seem easy enough, "Point to the noise, dummy!", but in reality, it was no easy task. With all the fog and the spinning of the boat, the foghorn sounded like it was coming from every direction - behind me, in front of me, over there - over here? I felt like I was a doomed character in *The Blair Witch Project*. To make matters worse, Kenny asked me for one of my anxiety medications. At the time I was taking Klonopin. It is a strong sedative. I told Kenny that under the circumstances I highly recommend that he not take this drug. He told me that he was so stressed out that he needed it to think clearly. I protested that it would not mix well with the beers he was rapidly consuming. Kenny kept insisting so I gave him a pill (.5mg, a relatively small dose) and went back to my post on the bow.

On cue about a half hour later, I felt the boat going around in small tight circles, spinning like a top. I went back to find Kenny shit faced, completely inebriated. He had a bewildered, drugged look to him. He had charts out all over the place and what looked like a sextant or some other primitive outdated navigational instrument. Kenny used to work in the Merchant Marine and took great pride in his chart plotting ability. I told Kenny that we were going around in circles for over an hour and voiced my concern that we might run out of gas. The tide was getting stronger and the wind was picking up. I told him I thought we should call the Coast Guard for assistance.

"Call the Coast Guard?" he bellowed with indignation, "the Coast Guard! I am not calling the Coast Guard! We are not in distress. You should only call the coast guard if you are in distress and we are not!"

He then handed me a piece of rope that was attached to his waist. He told me to tie it around my waist so if we hit the water we could find each other. Now I panicked. I would sooner tie myself to the anchor than attach myself to this drunken imbecile. For a moment, and only for a moment, I saw a knife sitting there on a bench and I thought to myself, maybe I should kill Cousin Kenny and call the Coast Guard myself, claiming self-defense. But Kenny was much stronger and tougher than me. I quickly, vividly visualized the torture he would put me through if I missed with the knife. Finally at daybreak the fog lifted a little and we hugged the shore back to the inlet.

On the way back home to Moriches, the next day, Kenny's boat broke down off Amagansett. He did not have SEA TOW (a service that cost about 100 bucks a year for unlimited towing) and it cost him close to a thousand bucks to be towed back to Moriches. Years later Kenny came to fish with me on my boat. He was in his final round of oxycodone addiction and was not good company, very chatty and delusional. He had lost probably thirty pounds. I had been trying to get him to fish with me for years but he always told me he had a "doctor's appointment that week." I remember thinking it odd how many doctors' appointments he had.

Like all guys abusing pain medication, Kenny was a pain in the ass. Kenny marked his arrival In the parking lot by honking his horn and yelling at Hank, the most easy going UPS driver you have ever met, who was apparently blocking the parking space that Kenny had designs for. Kenny then went on to loudly complain to anyone who would listen about the prices at the marina. After we loaded the boat with our gear he went and got a six foot heavy chain from his truck and proceeded to chain up the cart that was provided by the marina and free for boat owners to use. When I told Kenny that the chain was not necessary and asked him to unchain the cart, he looked at me and said, "what if the wind picks up?" If the wind picked up to the point of lifting up a cart while we were out fishing, the cart would have been the least of our problems. Sadly, that fall Kenny died in his sleep at his mother's home in Mastic-Shirley at forty-six years of age.

A few years went by; I continued to fish for stripers as much as possible. I logged many hours fishing the East River, along the FDR and under the Triborough Bridge. I only caught one bass in all that time. In the summer and fall I continued to go fishing with my friend Gary and his son Nick. They were great to me. I would often stay over at their nice warm house in Westhampton.

One day I got a call that the movie based on my book was going into production! This time I was to get a check for seventy thousand dollars.

Once again my very first thought was: now I can get a bigger boat and really fish; now I can move to Montauk and fish all the time. But first, maybe I could make more money. Now that they had name actors attached - Gretchen Mol (*Boardwalk Empire*) Jeff Garlin (Larry David's buddy in *Curb Your Enthusiasm*) and Sean William Scott, aka "Stifler' from *American Pie* - maybe I could sell my book, too. I shopped it around but got only rejection letters. One agent told me that the book had "no redeemable qualities" and I was unrealistically optimistic to think otherwise. Still I pressed on and eventually a twenty-eight year-old agent, Jarred Wiesefield, sold the book in two weeks at auction to Simon & Schuster for fifty-two thousand dollars. Now I had one hundred twenty-two thousand dollars to go fishing!

*

Captain Jeff Hits Montauk

Now, with the movie and book money in hand, I could buy a proper boat and really start to fish. Over that winter I took a crash course to get my captain's license. With a lot of hard studying and memorizing answers, I passed the captain's exam. A strong feat for this learning disabled man; standardized tests are like Kryptonite to the learning disabled. I did not tell anyone at first, except, of course, my mother, who acted as if I had passed the medical boards or law bar. It was good to have this under my belt considering my plans to run charters down the line. But first I needed to learn how to catch big fish. I need to put time in and probably mate on a charter boat to learn the ropes.

So the next spring I showed up in Montauk with a nice new little boat called an Angler. It was a middle of the road simple boat, but had a big cabin and lots of deck space or a huge "dance floor" as a friend put it, and all the electronics, the GPS, the fish finders etc. This was now 2003 and striped bass population had regenerated fully, thanks to a hard fought environmental movement articulated in Dick Russell's book *Striper Wars: An American Fish Story.* The fish were everywhere, and, because a particular commercial industry was recklessly harvesting tons of bunker a year to be used, among other things, as cat food and fertilizer, there was a lot less bunker (stripers' primary forage). The bass were ravenously hungry. On my second day with the new boat I put out an umbrella rig with wire line and within ten minutes I had two twenty-five -pound striped bass in the boat - on the same umbrella rig! I could not believe it. And this became the norm! I remember thinking to myself, "This is heaven! I cannot leave this wonderful fishing ground; I must do everything in my power to stay here."

When you first show up at Montauk, once dubbed "the sports fishing capital of the world," no one speaks to you. Maybe the town drunk will come up and bum a cigarette off of you. That's about it. It is almost remarkable in that way; here is a town that needs the tourist industry to survive and yet they were completely indifferent to tourists. When I first came to Montauk, Phil's Garage in the middle of town had a sign up that read "Locals Only." This attitude is changing, and (many feel) for the worse. Slowly, the fishing industry is being pushed out of Montauk. A couple of years ago the town of East Hampton, which includes Montauk, almost sold its public fishing docks to a private developer (translation: condos). Eventually, many feel that Montauk will simply be an appendage of the Hamptons. Like Harwichport, Massachusetts, Montauk will no longer be a fishing hamlet.

Now I was dead-set on getting one of those big forty pound plus bass that eluded Cousin Kenny and me in years past. I wanted my face on the front page of a fishing magazine. And now I had the resources to do it. I knew the boats and captains that were catching big fish. But they did not go out every night; they only fished on the strong, full and new moon tides. So instead I followed the commercial fleet around. They were nice guys and didn't mind so much. Some of them were old haul seine netters who were compensated by the government when their fishing tactics of pulling massive amounts of fish off the beach with nets were, for good reasons, outlawed. They were allowed to harvest a certain amount of fish per year by rod and reel and given out pliable metal strips called "tags" to be put in the fish's jaw and to document their harvest. The problem for me was that they were only allowed to catch fish no bigger than thirty-four inches and fished only in areas where market-sized fish were. I wanted to catch the slobs (giant stripers), which generally swam alone out of the strong currents were other smaller fish fed.

Eventually, I found the guys and the place where these monster fish were being caught. They only fished at night. I would get right behind these boats or as they called it, "mugged them." Even though I was close I never seemed to catch much. And they did every time! I would see these guys at the docks weighing their trophies in. No one spoke to me.

The next day I would watch these guys weigh in one forty-pound fish after another but I had been right beside them! How could this be? When I followed them too close they would purposely lead me to a place that held no fish, and pretend to put their lines down, but really just let the line out a couple of feet. When I would set up behind them and put my line to the bottom they would start the engines and leave. I knew one famous captain who used to fish with his lights out so no one could see him. One time I got smart, I pulled near him with my lights out too. I watched him closely. I could see pretty clearly under the light of the moon. When two of the guys hooked up on fish, I started my engine and headed right for him. I knew he could not pick up and move because they were tight on a fish. I simply went a hundred feet ahead of him and hit my GPS mark "MOB", man over board, and then I ran up on the other side of him and did the same thing. Now I had the exact coordinates within one hundred feet of where they hooked up on these fish. It turned out to be a subtle group of small boulders called the "The Slot" where big stripers lay.

Even with this location I still had problems catching slobs. I was hooking up on giant fish, but I was using "Fireline" (a Berkley braid) and for that you need to use a specific knot called a palomar or the line will slip. I did not know this at the time and certainly no one was about to tell me. So I would hook up with a big fish, go to set the hook hard, and the knot would slip. I would scream in agony and disbelief. Finally with the correct knot I started to catch big fish but was unable to break the coveted forty-pound mark. Lots of thirty-pounders and a thirty-five-pounder was my biggest. But I wanted a cow. Considering the amount of time I was putting in and the abundance of big fish around in 2003 it is amazing that I did not land a big fish....everyone else was. It was that easy. These were the glory days.

Now that I had the location it was only a matter of time. The entire summer I saw guys weigh huge bass, in the forty to fifty pound range. I was in awe of them; they were my idols. One guy, a captain named Jimmy George, landed a sixty-nine and one half-pound slob with a mysterious spoon he made by hand! There was talk that he planned to eventually sell the lure. But, even though everyone was talking about the "Secret Spoon" up and down the east coast, as of 2003 very few people had seen the lure that was landing slob after slob.

One of the many reasons why I was not catching big bass was that I was under the mistaken assumption that big bass were in the rips. The "rips" are where the water depth changes from, say, forty feet to twenty-five feet and then goes back up to forty feet. This disruption in the ocean floor pushes the displaced water to the surface causing visible waves or rip lines. These waves become bigger as the tide strengthens and wane as the tide weakens. Also, if the wind is against the tide the waves on the rip will stand up taller.

It is true a striped bass, being an ambush predator, likes to feed in these specific areas as bait fish such as peanut bunker, anchovies and sand eels, are helplessly pulled by the strong tide over the peak of the ocean floor to the awaiting open mouths of the stripers. All you had to do was present your bait across the bottom structure to get a strike by a fish between fifteen and twenty-five pounds.

But the "rips" did not hold larger bass because the current has to be moving very fast to dislodge the bait fish and pull them against their will over the structure. A huge striped bass simply is not willing to waste the energy fighting a strong 3-knot tide. A big fish would rather sit off by itself behind a bolder far away from the rips and the frenzied competing smaller stripers. Slobs will feed if something happens to come directly across the bolder they are behind. If not, they will wait for the tide to drop off a bit and then scavenge around some. It is said that a forty-pound striper will only feed for about a half hour of the six-hour tide, while a smaller fish will feed for three hours of a tide. All this varies depending on the moon cycle and strength. On a weak tide, for instance, you need to fish at the strongest part of the tide for all fish. On a big full moon tide, the big fish bite at the beginning and the end of the tides, or at the "book ends," if you will. I have never caught a forty-pound plus striper when the tide is moving faster than three knots. (1.7 to 2.0 knots is the optimal speed for slobs.)

Well, at the time, I did not know any of this... I just knew, and was told, that fish liked the rips and that they fed in the most pronounced area of the rips. Again, no one told me differently at the marina. No one told me that the slobs were not in the rips but out beyond them at places like the Slot, Great Eastern Rock and the Porgy Hump.

My friend Craig and I, on the night of the full moon in June, used to put on life preservers and head right to the strongest part of thunderous Pollock Rip. If it was an outgoing tide and the wind was ten to fifteen miles an hour out of the south west (which was common), there would be six to eight foot breaking waves awaiting us. Craig would drive the boat right into the waves and I, holding on with one hand to the hard top, would let the line out with the eel attached to it. Many times we would bury the bow of the little twenty-two foot Angler when we hit the first breaking wave of the rip, taking uncountable gallons of the sixty-degree seawater over her bow. We did not know any better; we thought this is how you fished Montauk. Every fifth drift or so we would get a bite, and sometimes, miraculously, we would land a small keeper striper.

One time driving back through the rip I looked back and got scared at the sight of the immense following sea that was steadily growing with the tide. How did it get so big? I panicked. I did not know what to do so I put the boat in neutral. This made the boat impotent and the huge wave simply picked us up and pushed us on our side probably one hundred feet. The boat was completely on its side, ready to capsize fully as the cabin was filling up rapidly with water. I was frozen with panic. Luckily, Craig, a more resourceful man than me, moved quick and hung his entire body over the side of the boat as if he were on a small sailing boat, and eventually, with the help of his considerable weight, the boat righted itself and flipped back on its bottom.

We still had massive amounts of water in the boat. I started the engine, which had stalled, and at least had the presence of mind to turn the boat to the south and head back into the oncoming breaking waves (after all, it is usually the second wave that gets you, I was told). Though we were heavily burdened with the weight of the water in the boat, we made it back though the rip. The boat began to drain and the bilge pumps dutifully kicked on as we limped back to Montauk Harbor. We both knew how remarkably close we were to drowning as it was nighttime and there were no other boats around and the water was cold.

I spent every day and every night fishing. I was hemorrhaging money, spending it like a drunken boxer. I exhibited little discipline. Rather than shop around for good deals on the internet and tackle shops up island, I bought all my gear, bait and tackle at the marina store at full price. While in Manhattan I went down to Paragon Sports, where I once worked, and spontaneously, and somewhat recklessly, bought five thousand dollars' worth of rods and reels. Some I needed, some I did not. I have none of them today.

I slept every night on my Angler. I loved it. I also valued the people at the marina, they were great folk. I never charged my friends to fish with me, and when they broke a rod I would buy a new one. On the off-season I continued to spend. Having a movie in production gave me access to a whole new world of dating. Before I sold the movie I was lucky to get one reply out of a hundred on Match.com. Now with money in hand I was by no means a playboy, but I was getting dates, particularly young Eastern Block women from Brooklyn. We would drive to Atlantic City, all expenses paid by Nichols Enterprises. (Believe me, when the money dried up, these women fled like a gazelle being chased by a lion.) I needed to get some revenue coming in soon. At this point I had not made the crossover from an enthusiastic sports fisherman to a fish mongrel...but selling fish for me was quickly coming up on the horizon.

Still I wanted to catch a big striped bass and despite my efforts it had not come to pass. I did not catch a fish over thirty-five pounds all summer and it was maddening. It was not until October 2005, that my friend Nick and I finally happened on a giant striped bass. We were fishing a famous spot called the Porgy Hump where Bob Rocchetta, in 1981, right before the striper collapse, caught the world record bass, weighing in at seventy-six pounds. (The record was broken the next year by Al McReynold's controversial seventy-eight pounder). We had not had much action all day, just a couple of small bass and a bluefish or two. Nick was only twenty-two at the time and was getting restless. I told him to calm down and have patience; we had to wait for the big girls to show up at the end of the tide just before it goes slack. As I said, on a full moon tide the big ones move around and pick up the scraps left by other fish. Well sure enough right before the tide slacked off, I heard Nick say quietly, "Jeff, get the gaff." I looked up and on the surface, about a hundred feet away was the fin and the big tail of a huge bass. Nick got her close to the boat pretty quick. At first I missed with the gaff, and the fish pulled out about fifteen feet of line to escape the boat. Nick worked her back, begging me not to miss again. I gaffed the fish. Eureka!

When the fish hit the deck we celebrated like we had just won the World Series, jumping up and down and rejoicing. All was right with the world. Nick was the angler yes, but the fish was taken on my boat; I knew how to be at the right place at the right time and this took a lot of work, practice and patience. Now I had broken the threshold. We were now big fish slayers. Going by the size of her as she lay on the deck, I knew she most have been close to fifty pounds. This is what I needed to launch my charter boat career! I knew a fish like this could end up on the cover of a fishing magazine - it did; *Noreast Oct 2005* - and I was going to get as much press as possible out of her. Sure, I may have spent much my life confined to a special ED class room, I may have failed as an athlete in school and flopped as a comic, but now I was a proven fisherman. I was very proud.

I refer to the fish as "she" and use "her" because slobs are female, which is one of the things to remember as I tell this story. At the dock Nick and I sucked in all the praise. Though it was not necessarily a remarkable fish (only a sixty-pounder will get people to raise an eyebrow in Montauk), it was still a big one: a "slob", a "pig," a "cow." The fish weighed in at forty-eight pounds, two pounds short of a fifty. I was in heaven and very happy for Nick. Then something odd happened. I was cleaning the fish with Nick at the cleaning station and a guy walks up to us. I expected the typical nice fish comment - where did you catch him? But what happened surprised me. He walked by me and said, "Nice fish, but you really should have released her."

I thought he was joking.

I asked him why. He told us that big fish were all females, that they were important to keep the species going as they laid a lot of eggs and were the top of their species. Throwing a trophy fish back at the time was simply inconceivable to me. Being the consummate wise-ass and wanting to impress Nick, I asked the guy:

"Let me ask you a question: how many eggs did this fish lay last year?"

He told me about 2 million. Then I asked him how many eggs this fish probably laid the year before that, he said about 2 million again. Then I belched, "Isn't that enough fucking eggs!"

Nick and I laughed like crazy and the man walked off shaking his head. Sadly at this point in my life I was not even close to being able to grasp what this good man was trying to convey to me regarding the importance of conservation.

Fools despise wisdom and instruction.

Proverbs 1:7

*

Andy "the Druggy" and How I Got Caught Up in the Black Market

Within the first thirty seconds of meeting Andy, he mentioned that he noticed that I had been catching a lot of nice sized striped bass, and asked me, with the same casualness as if he was asking me why I did not use WD-40 to lubricate my reels, why I did not sell my fish.

Feeling rather cool, I told him I had been unloading a few at a restaurant back west (meaning toward New York City). Realizing that I was now a potential scofflaw, he asked me what I was doing that night. Since it was not a full moon or new moon, hence a weak tide, I said, "Probably sleeping." It was then that Andy told me about his side operation. He told me that the price for bass was down and not worth the gas, but that in the harbor alone there was a goldmine of fish. You did not have to leave the harbor to make good money; sand eels, squid, silver sides (or, as the locals on the east end call them, "mummy chugs"), peanut bunker, spearing, and juvenile snappers were abundant. At low tide they would school up along the side of Montauk Harbor – hence the huge seine net on the front of Andy's boat. The huge, commercial-size net taking up the entire bow of the boat was certainly not recreational. Andy told me that I could make a lot of money working with him. Like I said, inconceivably I had blasted through the majority of the money I got from my film and book, so I was game for some income.

I am not entirely sure if "druggy," as he was sometimes referred to around the docks, was an accurate nickname for Andy. For, me at least, "druggy" implied a flop or a slacker like Jeff Spicoli from the movie *Fast Times at Ridgemont High*. While Andy did like his pot he was far too industrious and opportunistic to fit into my definition of a druggy. Andy had a good head on his shoulders. He was sharp and articulate and also had a great sense of humor. He was also, sadly, a horrific bootlegger and poacher of everything that swam. Andy did not have a "recreational" bone in his body. Anything that lived in the ocean Andy saw as a dollar sign and wanted to capture, kill, and then transport to his favorite market place: Chinatown, New York City. It should be known that while Andy was certainly a scofflaw, compared to what illegally submerged gill nets do in the Chesapeake and what the draggers are up to off of North Carolina, on the poacher spectrum, Andy was a very small player.

As it so happens, Andy's small skiff was in a slip a few boats down from mine. I was aware of Andy and the skiff. The boat stood out conspicuously compared to most of the sport fishing boats in the marina. It was not a sleek or sporty boat; there was nothing recreational about either the boat or Andy. The skiff, I think a Boston Whaler spin off, (maybe a Maritime skiff) was old and beat up. It was probably only eighteen feet or so with a small, maybe fifty-horsepower, outboard engine. In the front of the skiff, Andy had a huge anchor ball. An anchor ball is usually proof that a guy knows what he is doing. Very few recreational boats have anchor balls as they take some practice and labor to use. Once mastered, they can be great at getting the anchor off the bottom as the plastic ball absorbs the weight of the anchor rather than ones back.

Andy always walked around with a small dog and was probably a hair over 6 feet and had a splay-pigeon toed gait. He also, as I remember, always had his pants hiked up too far above his belly.

Andy wore white, rubber fishing boots all the time. Unlike me, Andy was not a trophy/ego hunter. Andy, like most commercial fisherman, was completely unimpressed by someone weighing in a fifty-pound striped bass. If he could not sell it he did not want it. Andy was not after bass over twenty-five pounds because restaurants did not want them. If a slob hit his hook, and over the years I am sure Andy encountered several, his only concern would be that it would be too big to sell. Restaurants in Chinatown would only give him a dollar a pound because much of the weight was head and backbone. Also, the meat is likely to be too tough. (Personally, while there are more PCBs in a big fish, I think they taste just as good as small bass. I prefer sea bass, blackfish, and flounder.)

Andy was a lifelong fisherman. He was acquainted with just about every fishing job there is. At forty-years-old he had never had any other job. He had worked on long liners, lobster boats and draggers for years. He had tried his hand at mating on charter boats, but found the customers too annoying. (I can confirm that being a mate on a charter boat is basically like being a waiter at a TGI Friday's, except that there are waves and people are puking and as a waiter you are not getting hit in the head with sixteen-ounce lead sinkers.) Andy wanted to make money on his own terms.

Andy was primarily a clammer on Long Island's Great South Bay. (Andy was a skinny, wiry guy, but as I said, never mess with a clammer or any guy no matter how small who does manual labor for a living. Anyone who rakes muck for eight hours straight is a strong son of a bitch.) When the market for clams dropped below a certain point, Andy would turn to crabbing. When the price fell off on that or the season was closed, he would go for flounder in Great South Bay. Tragically, the clam fishery was wiped out by over-fishing and something called the brown tide (spawned by over development/pollution.) Sadly, a lot of independent fishermen have been forced to leave fishing and get in line with everyone else filling out applications at the Home Depot or Walmart. Andy did not see leaving the sea as an option. He was defiant.

What brought Andy to Montauk were the words: "Six dollars a pound," the price that bass were fetching at the time at the fishing wholesalers. Andy was a licensed commercial fisherman and had "tags", 7-inch strips of pliable metal with numbers that were parsimoniously dispensed by the D.E.C. authorities. It was not easy to get these tags since striped bass were so regulated they were only given out to people who had been fishing for bass before the moratorium in the early 80's. There were all kinds of loopholes and stipulations in the system. For instance, fishermen were grandfathered in if they had been an East Hampton haul seine netter. The commercial draggers were also allowed a certain number of tags for their by-catch, but the D.E.C. tried to give the draggers just a few tags each so that it was not worth their while to target striped bass and wipe out the entire population again. (This number has been increased to twenty-one fish in NY State. There have been recent efforts made by commercial lobbies in 2012 to allow a group of commercial fishermen to go out on one dragger with a net and catch their entire allotment in one day.)

By law, a wholesaler or restaurant could not buy a bass without a metal tag in its jaws. And if the restaurant had fillets they better also have the rack that those fillets came off of. In hindsight, I now know, Andy's plan was to catch as many bass as possible, drive to Chinatown (his main consumer) and, if caught, show the tags and say, "Look, I forgot to put them in." Andy was not typical, as I have said, I know many pin hookers and Andy was the only knuckle head dumb enough to pull this move. All the pin hookers I knew were meticulous with their documentation on the fish they shipped.

A good prosecutor could probably convince any jury to have Andy shot for illegally trafficking our nation's sacred striped bass. But Andy had a certain charm about him. People liked Andy. He was funny and smart, and he could use this to his advantage. Also, just for a second, try to walk in Andy's shoes: he grew up seeing his father and friends living a relatively robust life as bay fisherman with no restrictions and minimal supervision, catching as much as they needed to. And now Andy and all the pin hookers, due to excessive regulations, had basically been asked to tie up their boats, put away their rods and go work at Burger King.

So what Andy proposed was that I would go with him for a couple of hours at slack tide, round up some of these small fish in his net and pack them into gallon plastic canisters. Then he would drive them off to Chinatown, where each canister would fetch $20. He told me that we could probably fill 50 canisters and we would split the earnings down the middle. I did some quick arithmetic in my head. I remember first asking Andy, "The Chinese eat fish that small?" Andy said that they eat all fish, perhaps making soup with it or something.

Intrigued by the adventure of it all, I told Andy I would go along. But I told him that it was far too much money for me for just a few hours; why didn't he just give me forty bucks? I would be happy with that; I could put it toward my gas bill. He told me not to be ridiculous that this was a "money run" and we would split it down the middle. I might make close to two hundred bucks, I figured.

So, in the middle of the night, at dead low tide, my alarm went off on my cell phone, I awoke and went with Andy along the banks of Montauk Harbor with a huge net, scooping up probably a couple of hundred pounds of small baitfish (mullet, mummy chugs, peanut bunker, spearing.) It was fun and interesting. The logistics are a little hazy, but from what I remember we embraced the fundamental principles of all netting of fish, including huge commercial operations, that is: find the mass of fish, round them up, and pull them in. However, unlike commercial boats of today, Andy did not have technology on his side (GPS, radar, fish finding instruments, etc.).

Andy's operation was a little more wholesomely primitive. Andy had me put on a pair of waders and dropped me off around seventy-five feet from the shore. He instructed me to wade through water four-feet deep pulling a rope attached to the large mesh net as I waded to the beach. He then quickly pulled the rest of the net around with his small boat. About fifty yards down the shore he stopped the boat and threw an anchor to keep the skiff from floating away. Then he too jumped in the water with his end of the net and headed for the beach. Once we both got to the beach, Andy told me to drag my end toward him, he did the same; we met in the middle. Then we both pulled the now heavy net up as far as we could on the beach. As we did so, I could hear the boiling baitfish in the nets.

This was really a microcosm of what the large commercial boats do. (Including netting endangered bluefin tuna in the Mediterranean.) As we dragged the "bag" onto the beach, I had flashbacks of when I worked on a commercial dragger myself. We were doing essentially the same thing, just with smaller nets and smaller fish. Then, right there on the beach, we started to pack them into the white plastic canisters. I liked the whole industry of it. This was old school. This is what civilization had done for centuries: pack out fish to be taken to market. How could this be wrong? Once we had loaded about fifty canisters or more into Andy's creepy, dilapidated white minivan, he was off to Chinatown. The problem with what Andy was doing, of course, was that if everyone did it the waters around Long Island would be completely barren of baitfish and the larger fish that depend on them to survive. Greece and Japan are great examples of how over fishing of bait fish destroys larger fisheries as well. General rule when it comes to all fish: No bait = no fish.

I went out alone the next day trolling for bass. When I returned I was surprised to see that Andy had not called me to let me know what the final "take" was. Andy did not return my call for a couple of days. Finally, I ran him down at the marina. I figured he would hand me the money right away, but he did not mention a thing, and simply asked me to hand him some things from the dock down to his boat. Eventually I asked him straight up for my cut. He was evasive, and then went on to tell me that, because the fish we netted that night were a "mixed bag" and not "pure" he did not get his regular price per canister in Chinatown. He said he had to go to a fish market in the Bronx to get a better price, but the "guy" was not there. As he handed me twenty bucks he went on and on about his overhead. "Look, I lost money on this deal," he pronounced. He mentioned the price of the plastic canisters themselves, and the price of gas, the tolls driving back and forth to Manhattan. All this made sense, but I did take note that he had not mentioned any of these expenses before the excursion. I knew my instinct to try and lock Andy in at forty dollars was right.

Anyway, Andy convinced me that the real money was in the striped bass once the price went up above three dollars. There were many nights when I could have taken ten fish, sold them all, and made a lot of money but I had too much respect for the fishery to do this. (I guess one will have to take my word on this.) Plus, getting caught with eight fish over the limit in a part of the country where the striped bass was as respected as the bald eagle would be far too humiliating, like the equivalent of selling cocaine at a middle school parking lot. It would make the papers.

One morning I was about to go out and catch my two fish limit (one fish over forty inches, one fish under) and take them to my "buyer" (my friend who ran a small caterings service on the East End) when Andy said, "Why don't you come along with me?" Of course I was reluctant after my last experience, but he said I could keep any two fish I caught and that I did not have to chip in for gas money. Also, he informed me, he had "commercial tags" so he would not have to go to Chinatown, but could sell right on the loading docks.

Far from being a fish bootlegger, I simply wanted to catch big fish, and I thought that perhaps Andy knew spots that I did not know about. Plus, he was a legitimate commercial fisherman; he had "tags."

Caught

Fishing with Andy was fun. He was bright and upbeat. While he was a good fisherman, he really did not know much about fishing technique in Montauk especially since he usually fished off shore on draggers or back west in the bays. His method of finding fish was like everyone else's: follow the rest of the commercial fleet. As I said, unlike me, Andy was not interested in any spots that held big or "trophy fish." Unlike most recreational fisherman, Andy did not have a huge ego. He just wanted to make money. Andy was the very definition of a fishmonger, someone who saw a fish only as a dollar sign.

Something about fishing seems to make people more candid and cheeky than they normally would be amongst relative strangers. Once we were anchored up "on the hook" and chumming for bass with mackerel chunks and waiting for the bite to begin, Andy told me he was married with kids. Then he told me that his wife was in the Asian massage business. I nearly spat out my soup on hearing that. He then went on to tell me that she had just turned forty and had switched over to the "managerial" side of things. Sensing my judgment, Andy followed his statement with a perfectly timed, "Look, I try not to think about it."

I could not help hitting the deck laughing. I was crying, howling, as Andy continued to fish. I was not necessarily laughing at Andy, just the way he delivered the info in such a matter of fact calm way as if his wife worked in a dental office. I was also laughing, I suppose, about how people get themselves into these predicaments. It struck me as cosmically funny.

As it turns out, I was not the only one Andy confided in. Andy had told others at the dock about his wife's occupation, and they all told him that he would make a killing if he brought some Asian girls out to Montauk. A bunch of the dockhands and some mechanics had convinced Andy that all the fishermen would sign up in a second. Well, sure enough within days, Andy showed up with about five Asian women, and walked up and down the docks with business cards that simply said "Asia" on them along with Andy's cell phone number. The card should have read, "Andy: clammer, fisherman, pimp."

Things did not work out as well as Andy had been ensured they would. All the people who suggested that he could make money all, quite literally hid. Someone ratted on Andy and he was thrown out of the marina. Undeterred, he brought his harem to the Montauk bar scene and was quickly chased out of town. Though Montauk was once the cocaine capital of Long Island, apparently they draw the line at prostitution.

Andy did return to Montauk, though, and we fished one more time together. He was only targeting bass now and claimed to be doing it on the up and up because he had commercial "tags". Andy was not using his little skiff but a big, ugly, recreational, 30 foot Bayliner; it was two-tone brown and had a soft deck. It was perhaps one of the ugliest pieces of shit that had ever floated in Montauk Harbor. The morning after a horrible night of fishing, during which we landed only four fish in the fog, Andy instructed me to pull two coolers (full of illegal fish that he had caught the day before with no tags) down the dock to his truck in the parking lot. Unsuspecting of foul play, I did not even think to look in the coolers. Andy was at the very least using me as a mule.

With a cooler full of ten illegal (untagged) fish I was met in the parking lot by Long Island's infamous Department of Environmental Control officer Joe Maffaro, AKA "Joey Boy." It is said that Joe wrote more tickets than anyone in the history of the D.E.C. Joe was a boy scout who was rumored to have given his own mother a ticket. When he and his posse invaded Montauk by land, sea and sometimes air, they turned the entire town on its head. Restaurants were closed, party boats given massive fifty thousand dollar fines and commercial fisherman tackled, handcuffed and hauled away.

When I first got to Montauk everyone talked about Joey like he was Darth Vader. I had never seen this man, but I was warned I would eventually and I would never see him coming...he would just appear. Everyone dreaded when Joey Boy pulled into town. He would often go out in a boat at night and use infrared binoculars to spy on unsuspecting fishermen. He was constantly in his car at the end of jetties waiting for boats to come in. When he saw one he was interested in (it was not unusual for it to be a boat that someone had complained about or ratted on), he would radio ahead to his posse and they would cut the boat off before it made it to its dock.

No one ever got away from Joey Boy. He was good at what he did, which was basically to get people to squeal on each other.

I know of one charter captain who had a group of people out even though his license had expired. He told the group beforehand that in the unlikely chance that they happened to be pulled over by harbor patrol or the Coast Guard, since he did not have his license, to tell the officers that they were just "friends" who were chipping in for gas. Of course, the customers all agreed to this...

As it turned out, the boat was indeed pulled over, and two minutes after Joey Boy stepped on deck they all sang like canaries and turned on the captain, saying that they were indeed paying customers. The best way of extracting the truth is through fear. Maffaro told the customers, after they weakly went through the motions of repeating the captains script: claiming that they were all just good "friends," that he knew it was a charter and that they had agreed to pay the captain a full fare, and if they did not admit it they would be guilty of obstructing justice and lying to an officer of the law. He explained that this is a crime with a possible twelve thousand dollar fine and up to one month in jail. Of course the customers sang.

Getting caught by Maffaro (or "Maffaroed") was a humiliating experience. It was a busy Saturday in the middle of the summer in the parking lot and the marina was full of people. Joey Boy was the first to get to me as I slowly made my way across the lot. He waved to me and called out my name (how did he know my name!?!). Officers in two D.E.C. trucks pulled up with sirens blaring and jumped out standing on both sides of me. The entire parking lot looked on at this growing spectacle. One guy had his hand on his revolver seemingly ready to whip it out if I made a bad move. Even before I saw his nametag I knew I had been nailed by Joey Boy. Some way, somehow, I was going to be Maffaroed! Did he know about the two fish I sold in East Hampton or about Andy and me dredging the harbor?

As Joey asked me to open the cooler, I looked at his badge and saw the name Maffaro it was HIM...this was Joey boy! He was tall, maybe 6' 2", with mustache and sunglasses. (In a funny way he kind of looked like that guy on *Reno 911,* on Comedy Central, with the short shorts.) I remember being asked to slowly empty my pockets, being a slob I always hated doing this. My pockets contain the usual debris of useless outdated receipts, lint, half eaten Snickers bar with maybe a quarter jammed into it, and maybe some inexplicable string or twine. I remember one officer mentioning what a slob I was. He hit that on the head!

The D.E.C. is a tough lot, a modern equivalent of rough riders or marshals. They are one law enforcement division I am told, that does not need a warrant to enter someone's home if they suspect an environmental violation, which is a wide umbrella. One guy's home was invaded because he had a deer rack and a turtle shell (that he found while on the beach) that had no documentation. According to the D.E.C. even a deer antler rack that was less than two years old needed to be documented. This particular guy had a lot of stress and embarrassment put on him and had to spend a lot of money on lawyers just to get a plea bargain settlement.

As the officers opened the cooler and I saw how many fish were in there, I too was surprised. I became very confident in my argument that we did not catch these fish, that they must have been caught the day before, or days before, and that we only caught four fish (two over our limit). Surely they would believe me. I was telling the truth about what happened! "Just look at the fish you can tell that we did not catch them today!" I protested. That was the truth. All of this fell on deaf ears. I basically got the old "tell it to the judge" from Maffaro. I felt so violated.

Maffaro then marched me down to find Andy. "You did not put those tags in!" Andy bellowed. File that one under nice try. Andy tried every move in the book. None of his protests worked. He did in the end try to get me off the hook by saying to Joe, "Come on, we don't have to involve him." referring to me. Andy was not a soulless man and we were friends. Joey's wolfpack then descended onto Andy's shitty Bayliner and ripped apart the boat. They found pot and God only knows what else. Andy could not even prove that the boat was registered to him. In fact I don't even think the boat was registered at all. The whole time Andy was pleading with the officers not to step on the deck too hard. He was scared the officers would put a hole through his dilapidated deck. Even under this stress I found that to be funny.

We were both given summons to appear in the conservative court of East Hampton. The games were about to begin.

An irony was that I was going to get some press from fishing, like I had always craved, but of course not the kind of exposure I wanted. This was my biggest fear: to be labeled a poacher when in reality I hated poachers. My friends can attest to this. Many times friends have asked me to keep an extra fish. Had I done it a few times? Yes. But most of the time I was adamant that we never go over our limit, if not for environmental preservation then to avoid this exact scenario: me ending up in the police blotter... Just like when I was in the comedy business and got caught stealing a joke, I was now in deep shit in a very conspicuous way.

This arrest was just the beginning of a long process of being exposed to a larger criminal element and network. I was the smallest cog in what was apparently a large black market fishing industry. Andy was a step above me. It seems that Chinatown was not the only place Andy sold to. Often, he unloaded fish to tractor-trailer drivers parked off Long Island expressways. The D.E.C. cops tried to get everyone to rat on everyone else. The D.E.C. told me, for instance, that they were really after Andy, as he was a repeat offender. If I testified against Andy I would get off with just a ticket instead of a misdemeanor and a write up in the paper. They then told Andy that if he led them to the trailers where he sold the fish he could keep his commercial license and pay only a two thousand dollar fine instead of facing two years in jail. And on and on it went; the domino effect.

As the court day was approaching I got a few calls from Joey Boy asking what I was going to do. What was I going to do? I was going to tell the truth; that I went out with Andy that night and we caught four fish. And that Andy asked me to pull down a cooler evidently full of fish that he had caught a day before, and that's what I got a summons for even though I did not catch any of those fish. That was the truth. When something goes wrong in my life, I try to slow everything thing down to low gear and be as honest as possible; it is just easier that way. Like the time I accidentally burned down my parent's family house with an old space heater, the house that had the 6 ½ pound brown trout above the mantel. That was a horrible situation, but when questioned by the insurance company I kept to the facts and I got through it. If you tell the truth you don't have to worry about mixing things up. You can tell the story over and over again from any angle or in any order and it comes out the same. I told Joe that I was glad that he caught us because I was beginning to sell fish on the side and did not want it to become a habit (which was true).

I then went on with the truth. That night on Andy's boat we only caught four fish. I should have never gotten a summons to begin with. I had no idea where Andy was selling the fish. (Which was true, I knew that Andy sold the baitfish in Chinatown, but I did not know where he was unloading the striped bass. I left out the fact that I had seen Andy several times load a cooler full of bass into his sleazy minivan, but that was his business.) I really felt that night that if Andy and I had caught a lot of fish he would have put the tags on the fish.

Still everyone around the docks seemed to be worried about me appearing in court. Every time I walked down the dock to get to my boat I would pass by some commercial pin hookers. "When is the court case?" They would ask. "You know a lot of people are concerned about you." I would kind of try and laugh it off, "Don't worry I don't have loose lips." Which is far from the truth; actually I love to gossip and I do have a big mouth.

One time a charter captain set me up. He asked me how the fishing was the night before. The night before I was fishing for striped bass at a place where some commercial guys liked to fish. There were smaller fish there that were inside their prescribed slot limits. The captain then asked me if I saw other boats out there. I said there were a few. I thought the guy was my friend but I had the presence of mind not to tell him what specific boats I saw or who the people were on them. But the damage had already been done. Later that day as I was filling up my boat with gas, I looked up and I saw two of the toughest looking commercial guys you've ever seen. One guy did the talking, "You have been shooting your mouth off about where we have been fishing and it is going to stop. If we hear that you shot your mouth off again, you won't be in Montauk very much longer."

I was fueling up to go over and pick up my girlfriend Kara in Connecticut, across the sound. The whole ride over I was in shock; why would that captain throw me under the bus like that? I guess these fishermen wanted the fish for themselves. What if the guys were stopped and boarded by the by the D.E.C. that night? I did not tell Joey Boy about these guys. As far as I knew they were doing nothing wrong. Was it safe to bring my girlfriend back to the docks? The whole ride back from Connecticut to Montauk I tried to put on a good front but I was pensive and upset.

The day came for our first court appearance. Everyone in the marina warned me that Maffaro would try to strike a deal with me on the side and that if I would not give him something else to go after - a restaurant or a boat - I would surely be sent off to Rikers. As I sat in the crowded courtroom Joey's head emerged from a door and he motioned to me. Again he asked me very pleasantly and calmly what I planned to do. (He had good manners; for some reason I wanted him to like me.) I said "tell the truth".

He then said, "Well, the truth is you know that Andy was selling fish illegally. That's all you have to say." He went on, "Look, Andy is going down no matter what. He is a repeat offender and other people will testify against him. There is no saving his license. But if you help me by testifying in the fall at Andy's trial, I will drop the trafficking charges against you and you walk away with a simple two hundred dollar fine." This offer did seem intriguing, I must say. I told Joey Boy I would think about it. I then went before the judge and pleaded not guilty to the charges and was appointed a public defender. I sat down and waited to see what Andy would do. I remember his head was lowered as the feisty but not unpleasant female judge reeled off a seemingly endless list of violations in front of a packed courtroom. With every violation the crowd, many of whom were there simply to deal with parking violations, ooh-ed and ah-ed. The book basically was thrown at Andy. Charges included, but were not limited to, possession of twelve untagged striped bass with intent to sell, unregistered boat, no proof of ownership of boat, expired commercial permits, intention to deceive government officials by not putting on tags, and possession of marijuana.

By the end of the list, half the courtroom was appalled, and half the courtroom was uncontrollably giggly at the spectacle of it all, at poor Andy's predicament. He actually tried to convince the disgusted judge that, through no fault of his own, he had fallen on hard times and that he was indeed NOT guilty on all charges. Andy's case was going to go to trial in the fall.

Andy disappeared from Montauk, although we spoke several times on the phone about the case. I went back to my primary purpose in life:

pursuit of giant striped bass. When the fall court date came up Andy somehow managed to get it pushed back. Little did I know that it would be another two years before this thing would be resolved.

*

Vinny: "Do What You Love and the Money Will Follow"

At the Marina I had become friendly with guy named Captain Vinny. Vinny had seen me hanging out with commercial guys like Andy and assumed I knew much more about fishing than I actually did and he offered me my first mating job. Vinny was a schoolteacher from Yonkers, NY, and might be the best example I know of a guy who extended himself too much when it came to fishing. I am sure it is no surprise to anyone that saltwater sport fishing is expensive. Even a small twenty-one foot center console can cost ten thousand dollars a year to run and maintain if kept at a marina. And the gear is intoxicating. I can sit back and imagine comedian Tim Allen from the 90's sitcom *Home Improvement* doing a sketch about fishing gear, acting out how fishermen become monkey-like in their excitement about a new GPS unit, or the latest high definition depth finder or a new high performance outboard engine. I have heard of people spending fifteen thousand dollars and more on a new radar unit.

Literally there are stories of people entering fishing tournaments on their child's college fund hoping to win the grand prize but losing everything. Can you imagine how you would feel if you spent one hundred thousand dollars on new electronics for your boat and then finding out that your nephew needs a major operation and you couldn't help him? This, of course, is an extreme case. But my point is this: if you want to get into recreational saltwater sport fishing, you better be well off.

Vinny was not your typical Montauk charter fisherman. He saw being a charter captain, like many weekend warriors do, as a chance to do what he loved and pretend it was a "business." In some cases, the only thing that separates a fishing bum from a captain is a piece of paper. In many cases a charter boat business is just a front, a tax right off; the "six pack" captain's license, a piece of paper to perpetuate the masquerade. Now a man can say to his wife, "Honey, I have to work." I can tell you from firsthand experience, a "six pack" captain's license is not all that hard to get. If you are lucky enough NOT to be learning disabled, sixty hours of hard studying, some clean urine (good luck finding that in Montauk) and no D.W.I.'s and you're in. But why? It can't be stated enough; there is no money in the charter fishing business! There is simply too much overhead. There may have been money in the business twenty years ago, and maybe there is some money left at tourist destinations like Cabo, Mexico, and Costa Rica. But on the eastern seaboard it is a dead industry. The busiest captains might make seventy thousand dollars a year profit. Most make enough to pay for their boat slip and storage, which seem to go up 20 per cent every year.

Also the charter business has dropped dramatically over the years. Charter fishing industry is the product of a strong middle class. If the middle class is making money and there are fish around, people will come to fish. Between the recession, excessive fishing regulations imposed on sport guys (NY state for instance, only allows twenty porgies; it used to be sixty, and three fluke to twenty-one inches; it used to be seventeen. In Florida you can't keep grouper or yellowtail or really anything), and the fact that gas prices have almost tripled (right now $4.56 at my marina), divorce and other activities that vie for customer's attention, i.e. paint ball, video games, the all-consuming internet, it is a wonder that one charter boat leaves the harbor. People just don't go fishing anymore.

Despite all this, Vinny, a schoolteacher, decided to go out and buy the most expensive sport fishing boat he could find. A completely outfitted thirty-five foot Cabo Express (three hundred seventy thousand dollars.) Then he went out and bought a full set of Penn International rods and dumped any money he had left (probably ten grand) into advertising. "Fish on a Deluxe Cabo Express..." the ad read in all the fishing magazines and websites. I have always said that the guy who wrote that book, *Do What You Love and the Money Will Follow,* should be beaten with a stick. Vinny confided in me that in his third year of chartering he made seventeen thousand dollars. His expenses were thirty thousand.

The story of how Vinny acquired the boat became a popular story for a while on Long Island. Apparently he told his wealthy Wall Street wife that he had designs on buying the craft. She, knowing that Vinny did not have a huge salary as a Westchester schoolteacher and had no money in the bank, jokingly stated that, "He couldn't even come up with the deposit for a boat." Well, Vinny did come up with the deposit by borrowing fifty grand from his father, and then fraudulently signed his wife's signature as a co-signer. When the wife found out she went ballistic and had him arrested for fraud. That very weekend was Vinny's parents' fiftieth wedding anniversary. Vinny's wife showed up with the two kids and no Vinny. "If you want to see him he is in jail," his wife, a decent person, explained. No one believed this story until Vinny passed around the police blotter in his local paper that documented the arrest. She eventually dropped the charges.

Caught

Unlike other captains with huge distorted egos, Vinny was in it for the fun. He was very laid back. Having fished with him several times as a mate, I can attest I never saw a trace of that ego that other fisherman had. He was in fact the opposite of the egotistical fisherman. One time as his boat left the entrance of the harbor a customer asked Vinny: "So captain, were can we go to catch large striped bass?" Without skipping a beat, Vinny replied nonchalantly and candidly, "Probably on another boat." This kind of self-deprecating humor made Vinny beloved by many. One time a well-known charter boat was trying to push Vinny off of a blackfishing spot. The other charter boat captain was intimidating and no one ever messed with this guy. He got on the radio and said, "Hey, Jane's Grace, who the hell do you think you are?" Vinny yelled back, "I am Captain Jack Sparrow!" Well, you get the idea. Vinny was not flawless, though. While he was humble about his fishing ability, he was a "gear head" - that is, he was addicted to high-end equipment.

In 2003 I occasionally worked for Vinny as a mate. About that time Captain Jimmy George began selling his "Secret Spoon," which caused much intrigue and fanfare on the docks. People were intimidated by Jimmy's spoon because you had to troll it at a certain speed and use a certain rod, etc. Naturally, Vinny wanted the lure for his boat. On one charter we had an eighty year-old man, his wife, their kids and their two grand kids, the whole family. The eighty year old had never landed a big striper so Vinny bought one of Jimmy's Secret Spoons at around a hundred twenty-five bucks, and got the old guy all excited about the prospect of catching a trophy striped bass. Vinny did all but guarantee him that on this particular day this particular lure would land a forty plus pound bass for him to hang over his fireplace. The man, perhaps not the brightest fellow who ever walked the earth, was very excited.

We went out and fluke and porgy fished a bit just to get some small fish in the boat and bend the rods, all the while Vinny kept fueling the flames, "Pops, you getting ready to catch the fish of your lifetime?" he said. The air was thick with anticipation.

The whole time I was rolling my eyes. First off, when taking a charter out, even in the best of circumstances and conditions, one must curb their enthusiasm until the fish is in the boat. So many things can go wrong out there. Plus, while Vinny did have the correct rod and rod holder for the spoon, I knew that Vinny only had a vague idea of where big fish lay and at what part of the tide they would bite. On top of this he had no idea how to troll a big spoon like Joey's. There is a lot to presenting the lure and making it swim correctly so the big striper will find it attractive; anticipating tide and current is one example.

So after a few hours of fluke fishing it was time for the eighty-year-old (a nasty old geezer) to catch his trophy fish! I went to put out the line in front of the entire family, who were sitting in chairs three feet behind watching me with great interest and enthusiasm. As I began to put out the line I noticed that Vinny was moving the boat too fast, around six knots, when he should be going about two knots. As a result, rather than sink beneath the water, the four-pound spoon started to skip or hydroplane across the surface of the water. When I yelled to Vinny that he was going too fast he simply waved and motioned to me to put it out further.

Making matters worse, Vinny had attached too big a swivel to the eight foot mono leader connected to the Secret Spoon, causing the swivel to lodge in the top guide, or eye, of the rod and not allowing any more line to go out. I gave it one firm tug to try to release it. This can work with lighter stuff, but in hindsight I should have reeled the lure into the boat and put on another swivel. Instead, when I pulled on the line, already stressed by the ridiculous speed of the boat and the weight of the lure, it snapped. The Secret Spoon immediately sunk to the bottom of the sea.

I looked back at the customers - the children, the grandchildren, the grandfather and mother who were all oblivious to what had just happened. They were still looking at me with great anticipation. To them it was not a matter of if we were going to catch a fifty-pounder but when. They did not know that the Secret Spoon, the very lure that was to capture this huge fish – "Grandpa's fish" - was gone before it was even let out. No longer connected to the line, the Secret Spoon was now resting on the ocean floor somewhere, and I certainly did not want to break the news to them. It was exactly like that popular commercial when someone screws up and the voice over asks "Want to get away?" I sat there for a full minute pretending to be still letting the line out, although I knew that this was an absurd exercise in avoidance; I had to face the music at some point. I finally screamed past the customers up to Captain Vinny that the lure was indeed gone. The old man was not going to get his trophy fish after all.

To say that everyone was disappointed was a huge understatement. I heard a lot of, "What?" and, "You're kidding me!" Vinny, of course, like all good captains blamed me, the mate. I tried to explain why it happened, that Vinny was moving too fast and about the big swivel that did not pass through the top eye of the rod but it was futile. No one gave a shit; I was the reason the spoon fell off and grandpa did not get his trophy fish. The day was ruined. I just tried to fiddle about the cabin to occupy myself for the long ride home.

I overheard the old man say to Vinny, regarding me, "Why did you even bring him?"

On a sad note, and one not related to fishing, Vinny passed away in 2008, due to heart complications he had had for years, at the age of fifty-four. I did not go to the funeral in Yonkers, but it must have been packed.

*

In Search of a World Record - Captain Jimmy George

Though Captain Jimmy George, the aforementioned inventor of the "Secret Spoon" and the guy who landed the 69.85 pound slob and was on the cover of all the magazines, had never said so much as a word to me on the docks, I once handed him a piece of tuna I had caught on another boat. It was a neighborly/political gesture. I believe he may have grunted "thanks." But there was no real eye contact, or recognition. The interaction was like feeding a piece of meat to a grizzly bear, or great white shark; they will take your offering, but don't expect a lot of praise afterward.

I guess he asked around about me because that winter I got a call from him. I did not recognize the number so I let it go to voice mail. "Hello, this is Captain Jimmy George," he said. "Jeff, I need a full time mate next year, and I think you would be good. Give me a call." For me this was the equivalent of being called up from the minor leagues or Sean Penn calling a no-name actor to play a role in one of his films. I was thrilled. Jimmy's boat, The Nicole Marie, was the hottest in the harbor. The year before no one caught more trophy size bass than Jimmy, and he was using the mysterious secret lure he made by hand. When I called back he wanted to know if I really had a captain's license. I said I did. He then asked me to fax it over. He said that he had a bad back and wanted another licensed captain on the boat for insurance reasons. I did not care what the reason was. It would be great; I would learn a lot and make a ton of money. I knew the mate who worked for Jimmy the year before and he had made close to thirty grand in four months. I was entering the big leagues. I also felt safer; Jimmy was a bad motherfucker and if he was my friend no one would fuck with me, not even the D.E.C. Maybe even Maffaro and the Boys would leave me alone now.

In the relatively tiny world of trophy striped bass fishing, nothing personifies fishing addiction like the story of Jimmy George, a flat-out living legend in the striped bass world. He is loved by some, hated and feared in a very real way by many, but his work ethic and passion for the sport has to be recognized and respected. Jimmy was also a great marketer and gifted storyteller.

I was the mate on Jimmy's boat from 2007 to 2009. We sailed just about every day, sometimes three trips a day. I spent a lot of time with Jimmy, dealing with his many moods and a certain guillotine of a lure, that "Secret Spoon" – the four-pounds of steel he fashioned himself with a custom 4X treble hook that he obsessively sharpened every ten minutes. In bad weather I had to try to retrieve this thing as it swung off the stern like a weapon out of a horror movie set in medieval times.

At his best, with his wonderful wit, rugged good looks and charisma, I am certain that if Jimmy were on the fresh water bass circuit, with all the sponsorship and prize money, he would be worth millions today. But as this story will attest, trying to get rich via striped bass is next to impossible. Truth be told, Jimmy could have been great at most anything he put his mind to. He could have been a brilliant dentist or even a surgeon. He was great with his hands, and his ability to concentrate was remarkable. He had such a commanding presence I bet he would have been a successful stand-up comedian. I'm not just saying this for obligatory reasons, but the fact of the matter is Jimmy George is bad ass.

In the mid-seventies, a time when the general public was in the dark about how sharks were becoming endangered, Jimmy, then a twenty-six year-old truck driver, landed the largest mako shark in US history weighing in at one thousand thirty-nine pounds. (The record has since been broken.) This shark landed Jimmy in the headlines of every major newspaper on the east coast. Adding to the hype, the movie *Jaws* had just come out, and Jimmy was viewed as something of a hero. The Daily News had a caption below the picture of Jimmy sitting on top of the head of the giant toothy shark with his tan chiseled muscular body, broad shoulders and movie star good looks, "Paterson truck driver catches dangerous man eater." Swarms of people admired the catch and the fisherman. What wild times they must have been. There could have been a parade down Main Street in East Hampton (or any Long Island town).

Today such a catch would not make the major papers, and if it did it would be portrayed in a negative light. Recreational shark fishing is discouraged, as it probably should be, even though it is not the main contributor to the massacre of sharks. Most of us know by now that as a result of what commercial long liners are doing and the insatiable, growing demand for shark fin soup in Asia, some species of shark face flat-out extinction. The overall population is down, some biologists believe, by 90 percent. I am told that in the 1980's off Montauk one came across several species of sharks: brown sharks, duskie sharks, and hammer heads. Now all you see are blue sharks, thresher sharks and the rare mako.

Caught

Catching this big shark and getting all of the adulation and fame may have been the worst thing that could have happened to Jimmy. After all, wouldn't all this notoriety go to most of our heads? But any glory from saltwater fishing costs dearly. The overhead is just too much (bait, tackle, gas, storage, slip rental, upkeep, electronics) for the regular guy to participate in this sport. There is a minimal TV audience and while there is huge money to be made in fresh water bass tournaments (much less overhead and more accessibility to the average man) from prize money and sponsorship, there was not much to be made with ocean fishing. The busiest hardest working charter boat captain might clear seventy grand a year...that is if he is lucky enough to avoid a major setback (like in my case, a blown engine.)

Jimmy was born in Paterson, New Jersey. His father was Lebanese and his mother was Dutch. Paterson was and still is a rough town with a high crime rate and typical inner city problems. Jimmy went to a predominantly black school, and as a child he was relentlessly picked on until he learned how to fight. Jimmy was a product of his environment. There is no way to sugarcoat it: Jimmy kicked a lot of ass in his day. Fishing was at first a healthy alternative for Jimmy. As a child he used to fish with his mother in the Passaic River for carp and catfish. He remembered his mother showing him how to make the dough they used for bait look dirty and natural. He had a big carp on once, but it got away. However, Jimmy saw the fish and the fishing bug bit. He worked hard all week, but once the weekend or vacation time came, it was all about fishing.

In the beginning, fishing kept him away from a criminal life. From May through November Jimmy was obsessed with fishing, always escaping to Montauk. Aside from catching big fish, he had a way with words. I found all his stories mesmerizing. From gang fights and stick-ups to catching huge fish, Jimmy's tales topped everyone's. If you try to tell Jimmy a story, you better make sure it's a good one, and chances are yours will not compete. I don't know how many times I would start to tell Jimmy a story, "Hey, Jimmy, so me and Joe went out and we hooked into this two hundred pound mako and..." In the middle of telling it I would realize by comparison how lame the story must sound and stop in mid-sentence.

Brimming with charisma and natural charm, Jimmy was and is a great fisherman. But like everything in life, luck always plays a part in catching a huge fish. I have learned this simple fact over the years: no matter how good an angler may be... if the fish ain't a there you ain't a catchin'. I guess the winning mix is preparation, skill, and luck. Perhaps Jimmy would have been served well by adding a little humility. Instead, he tended to a have a pompous air about him, a certain smugness that put some people off. Jimmy would walk around Montauk the way I imagine a bullfighter walked around Madrid in the 1930's.

Right after landing the record fish, Jimmy tried his hand at running a charter business. While he did well, he knew, for all the aforementioned reasons, that no matter how busy or good he was, he couldn't make a fortune in charter fishing. He left Montauk to run a successful trucking business and started a family. (Jimmy was a great family man. I have met his kids; they are great.) He still fished on weekends, and Montauk and the ocean were always on his mind.

The place simply called him. Thirty-two years after landing the huge shark, Jimmy, always an inventor and a scientist (and also a licensed pilot – a very hard test), tried out his new heavy steel lure in his swimming pool in New Jersey. He had made it by hand in his garage. It looked like a fluke or a flounder and cut through the water like a dart. Jimmy used the principles of aerodynamics that he learned as a pilot (speed of boat related to the strength and direction of tide) to make the lure swim as naturally as possible. Jimmy caught his 69.85-pounder on the spoon, touching off a media frenzy and again landing him on the cover of all the fishing magazines. In 2005 the spoon landed seven fifty-pounders and close to a hundred forty-plus pound fish.

Obviously this slaughtering of breeding bass disgusted many fishermen and environmentalists, but in Jimmy's defense, there was not as much information in 2005, about the importance of returning big fish, as there is today. For the most part, his accomplishments were applauded and admired. Think about it; while most sport fishermen simply use store-bought lures and bait or, like me, dunk live bait into the water (in my case eels, which because of Asia's demand for them and manmade dams, are also an endangered species), this guy Jimmy took a four pound slab of metal and fashioned a lure unlike anything seen before. Yes, in 2004 he was fishing at probably the pinnacle of the striper boom. Let me reiterate my simple premise yet again: in order to catch big fish, big fish have to be around.... But these big fish were attracted to Jimmy's lure because it was different.

On top of his work ethic and creativity, Jimmy was a great marketer. He didn't try to sell the spoon right away but rather let the suspense build. For the next two winters he pounded them out in his garage near Paterson, to the point that he got carpal tunnel syndrome. He painted and detailed them with an elaborate system worthy of a Detroit assembly line. I had the privilege of visiting Jimmy at his home in Little Falls, New Jersey, and I was amazed at what I saw. It was sheer industry. He cut the metal, pounded it out by hand, welded it, spray painted the spoon and then gathered them in a huge oven. Later when he was selling them, demand was so high at one point that he needed another oven. So he cut a hole through his garage wall and into the back of his kitchen, where he put a duct from the stove to the garage. As a "clinically un-handy" person, I'm impressed by anyone who can hang a painting correctly, but even the handiest among us would be impressed by Jimmy's skill, ingenuity, and sedulity.

Half of Jimmy's house was dedicated to the manufacturing of these spoons. All the while the buzz built and resonated. Jim really did keep it a "secret". Allegedly, a captain from a well know nighttime charter boat approached Jimmy and said that he would give him three thousand dollars on the spot for just one spoon. Other Montauk charter captains, a tight-knit fraternity, pretended that they weren't interested in the "Secret Spoon", professing that it was simply another variation of a bunker spoon. That may have been the case, but I remember a lot of customers on other charter boats staring slack jawed as we landed one big fish after another. Often other well-known charter boats would have to move their trolling areas to prevent being embarrassed by all the action on the Nicole Marie.

From 2006 to 2009 Jimmy had the busiest boat in Montauk. He used huge nine-foot custom rods that he ran out of extended rod holders. His reels were mostly Penn 4/0's, or International 50W's, and were clipped to a safety line. Just the gear alone, including the wire line, must have weighed twenty-five pounds. Let out three hundred yards of wire line, add a four-pound spoon dragging through the water, and then add Montauk's strong currents, the speed of the boat and a fish! All this pressure made it incredibly hard for me to even get the rod out of the rod holder to hand it to the customer. I could barely hold on to the rod *without* a fish on it. God forbid a fish hit the lure. A few times I had to ask a stronger customer to pull the rod out of the rod holder for me. Or worse, Jim had to leave the helm, push my sorry ass out of the way, and pull the rod out with one jerk. Once when I started working for Jimmy and I had barely gotten the rod in the rod holder after the third fish, I remember thinking, "Please, in the name of God, don't let a fish hit this fucking lure again!" And God forbid if Jimmy, who always had his eyes riveted on the tip of his port side rod - he controlled the speed and direction of the boat by observing how the tip was undulating - thought the spoon was swimming the wrong way or weeded up. (He controlled the speed and direction of the boat by observing how the tip was undulating - like a dog completely focused on a treat.) I would hear, "Jeff, reel that spoon in and check it for weeds!" Many times we would snag the spoon on a hundred-pound submerged lobster pot. Getting it back was dangerous to say the least. We would hand-pull the pot in as far as possible until we saw the leader, then work the lure free. If the huge custom built sharp 4x trouble hook grabbed on to you somehow, one would plummet down with the lobster pot. There would be no saving you. Someone died by getting caught in a lobster pot line three years ago in this very manner right in front of his horrified crew. I always wondered if Jimmy would continue fishing right after such a thing occurred.

When the "Secret Spoon" did come out it sold well. One charter boat in Connecticut did so well with the lure that the captain purchased twenty of them in one order. But when it came time to get a patent and hopefully sell the lure to a bigger distributor, things didn't pan out. Perhaps the lure was too similar to a bunker spoon to warrant a patent. Also many people do not like to troll wire line. By then, too, recession, restrictive fish limits and high gas prices were devastating the Montauk charter industry. Asians and Russians and others who used to "meat fish" Montauk started to go to Jersey and Connecticut because they were easier to get to and had higher bag limits (like seven fluke to two).

By 2010 Jimmy had only a smattering of customers. He admits that he could have done a better job keeping up with his client list: newsletters, phone calls etc. In many ways Jimmy didn't seem his old self. A few times he heard charter boat captains speaking poorly of him on the radio and he went crazy. A huge, intimidating man right out of a Melville novel, he got into verbal fights with other captains and Montauk locals. He wasn't afraid to raise his fists either, and fight dirty if he had to. No one wanted to mess with Jimmy. At times, the high-spirited, vivacious, storytelling Jimmy was all but gone.

But during the good years customers flocked to him from all over the world. As his mate I was learning to work hard and spent a lot of hours at Jimmy's side while we changed the oil or installed new gas lines or a GPS or radar dome. One time, bad back and all, Jimmy tried to load a generator onto the boat by himself and it fell over the side. We spent the day pulling it off the bottom, taking the entire thing apart and blow-drying the parts. We put the entire thing back together, but just when we thought we had finished we found an internal bolt that we missed. Some would have simply overlooked this, but Jimmy, ever the perfectionist, took the whole generator apart and put it back together again. We started the generator and it ran fine. We let it run while Jimmy and I sat up by the store at the marina relaxing after all our efforts. Suddenly we noticed smoke coming from the boat dock. We ran down to find the generator on fire. We blasted the flames out with a fire extinguisher and then just sat there and laughed hard. What else could we do?

Probably the best thing I learned from Jimmy was to stay calm at all times. Jimmy never got crazy on the boat. The crazier things got the calmer he would get. For example, he showed me how to take my time with a gaff, to wait for the fish to present itself before you struck at it.

Caught

If it was a full moon, after we put the Nicole Marie away, I often went off on my own boat and fished right through the night. I would come in, tie up my boat and leave the two fish I caught in a cooler on the boat. Later a guy who ran a catering service in Sag Harbor would drive all the way out and pick them up, leaving me a couple of hundred dollars under the empty cooler. I would then walk down to The Nicole Marie and start setting out the rods and readying the cabin for the morning trip. Often the customers were already there. Many times I went twenty-four hours without sleep.

I remember during this time we caught a couple of fish with peculiar red dots all over them, like chickenpox. Someone told me at the dock that it was a dangerous bacterial disease called mycobacteriosis... at the time it meant nothing to me. More on this later.

During this time, while I was working for Jimmy on the Nicole Marie, my book came out. My publicist at Simon & Schuster arranged a bunch of phone interviews. I was to call in to radio stations. I missed all but one. My publicist was not amused. I was always fishing. They were mostly all small markets. At the one station I did reach, in Delaware, the interviewer had not read a page of the book. It just felt silly describing it on the phone from a cabin of a boat.

Howard Stern had read an article I wrote for *Penthouse* about my demise in comedy and he tried to get me on the phone. This was one call I didn't want to miss. I was given a date and time when I'd go on his show. Howard's self-deprecating style had provided me with pleasure for so many years I could not wait to talk to him. I was tired and nervous when I took the call on the Nicole Marie. I had fished all night, but this was a good time. It was quiet at the marina. I was going to nail the call; I knew I was a funny motherfucker and he would love me. I had been told that with all my quirks and tics, I fit the profile of his entourage. I was sure we would hit it off and I would become a regular on his show and get all the women I wanted.

Howard's producer the great Bobba Buoy called and instructed me to hold for Howard. I heard a bunch of commercials then Howard came on. Somehow, inexplicably, the conversation got off on the wrong foot when I asked Arty Lange Directly if he had ever stolen a joke. Most comics have, but like steroids, no one ever admits to it. The question threw Arty off. There was some "Well, it depends..." Then they all took a defensive stand. Fearing I was about to get hung up on, as so many did, I started to speech blast them. I tried to push my book and movie and fishing business. Howard indulged me a little but basically hung up on me. I was mortified and angry at a blown opportunity.

Anyway, things were going well for Jimmy until the unthinkable happened. Around 2008, big fish abruptly stopped hitting the Secret Spoon. Perhaps they got used to the lure, perhaps as some feared, many big fish got wiped out in 2004-2006, the best years in striped bass history. Or maybe because there was more bait around, like bunker schools, and the fish did not have to take the chances they once did. As quickly as they had turned on to the lure, they rejected it. In 2010 you could literally rub the dust off Jimmy's spoon in fishing stores. They were an anachronism, from a different time and place. I used to joke with Jimmy that I saw one of his "Secret Spoons" on sale for $2 on a blanket on the lower East Side of Manhattan next to an old toaster and used VHS videos. It was almost the truth.

My memories of Jimmy George are solid: coming back with a boat full of yellow-fin tuna, gulls gliding behind the stern of the Nicole Marie, Jimmy telling stories and preaching religion to the satisfied and happy customers as Bob Dylan's *Tangled Up in Blue* blared through the speakers. But most of all there was his big laugh. I remember sitting with his family while he told stories and did impressions – Jimmy, his kid and wife and I all roaring with laughter. Jimmy and his wonderful fun family is exactly the type you want in your comedy audience.

Good friends we made...good friends we lost along the way.

*

Going Off On My Own with Second Choice Charters

The next year I felt I had learned enough about fishing Montauk to try chartering on my own, so I took out ads in *The Fisherman* and *Noreast* magazines and put up a website called www.secondchoicecharters.com. This benign and self- deprecating shingle was designed not to offend the other charter boats and, of course, Jimmy George. Jimmy was great with it at first. I used to joke with him that I was going to take out an ad that read: "Second Choice Charters: Fish Jimmy George's Numbers at Half the Price!" ("Numbers" referred to the coordinates where he caught his biggest fish). I focused on night fishing only. Customers did begin to trickle in and, truth be told, I did poach a few of Jimmy's whom I had become friendly with. The fact was that during the summer night fishing was generally better than daytime fishing, so it came naturally.

I should add that fishing at night on Block Island Sound is gorgeous. Fourteen years in a row, six months out of the year, I was blessed to witness the sunset and the sunrise. Some nights out on the sound it is so dark that the stars literally look like diamonds on a jeweler's black cloth. Added to this beauty is the adventure of taking a little boat out at night in the elements. How neat it is to see the topography of the ocean floor with all its ridges and valleys recreated on your sonar depth finder. Then the thrill of a big fish hitting your bait, "the wack", and screaming off with the line. Trying to contain the fish, trying to hold it away from the bottom where she might break off on a rock. All this contributed to the experience. To me, it's just great fun and after fifteen years of doing it, it still gives me goose bumps just thinking about it.

I remember coming into the harbor once after a great night of fishing and thinking how truly lucky I was to being doing this, at this time in history when striped bass was so remarkably abundant. I couldn't think of anything that was cooler than being a fisherman, except a rock star. Let's face it; rock star trumps everything. But short of that fishing was it; no one could be having more fun than me, I thought. I knew some actors, and while they love the fame and notoriety (not to mention the hot chicks) the work itself is often tedious and laborious - shoot after shoot, retake after retake. It is not all about the glory in that field. And writing, from the little taste I got of it trying to write this book, is a downright agonizing labor: edit after edit, fact check after fact check. We all glamorize Hemingway's and Fitzgerald's life styles, but these were hardworking men; no different than a dentist, roofer or plumber tediously laboring away at their craft. And to think, those guys did not even have Microsoft Word to help them.

The greatest striped bass story I know is from a guy named Charles Church who in a rowboat on high, dangerous seas by Cuttyhunk in the Elizabeth Islands landed a seventy-three-pound bass, a Massachusetts state record that still holds today. I have his story posted on my website. It makes me proud of people who surfcast, and fish in kayaks and try methods for catching bass that don't involve burning massive amounts of fossil fuel. If Charles Church did it, why can't we? Anything is possible if you use the tide to your advantage, people have rowed 15 foot boats across the Atlantic. My girlfriend used to get mad at me when I suggested I take my boat fifty miles from Montauk to Cape Cod where she lived saying it was too dangerous. Meanwhile my grandfather and his friends at the age of seventeen entered a five-hundred mile race around Bermuda on a twenty eight foot sail boat with only the stars to guide them.

*

The Up Side of Charter Fishing

As a charter boat captain, it is so easy to get caught up in the ego stroking aspects of catching big fish and "producing" for the customers. It is easy to forget about what's it really all about. Once in a while even a knucklehead like me experiences an access of sentimentality. Usually it's a subtle perception: the way one guy made sandwiches for the rest of the group, or how a trip won't leave without a particular guy in the boat. Or the Russian guys. I particularly liked the Eastern Block people who show up with their coolers and quiet optimism, happy to be able to spend the day on the water. How can your heart not go out to these people? I feel men are often at their best on the water. Sure there is laughter and joking around but also genuine concern for one another. The father and son trips rip your heart out the most. Some fathers try so hard to pass something along (like their father probably did for them) and hoping and trying to instill the fishing bug. Others are more laid back, just seeing what will happen out there. Sometimes it works and sometimes it does not.

As the captain, I always liked talking, sometimes months beforehand, to the person who is putting the trip together because I had been in their shoes before. We all have. They have to book the charter, put down a deposit and really put some skin in the game. They have to worry about whether the weather is going to be okay, about who might get sea sick... and get the group together. They have to hope everyone shows up on time and that the fishing is good.

Not only have I had the privilege to witness natural beauty: sunsets, sunrises, whales, dolphins etc. But I have also seen some human stories unfold. Four young guys (probably in their mid-thirties) chartered me once. As I saw them walking down the dock I noticed they all had rods. Now as a rule I don't like when people bring their own rods no matter how expensive and good they are (Loomis, St. Croix). I have a simple set up that works. It is tried and true: Penn 4/0, with fifty-pound mono and Penslammer 6.6' rods. Not the most expensive equipment but uniform and perfect because they are stiff and can handle up to the sixty ounces of lead weight needed to get to the bottom in the strong Montauk current. The rod also should be stiff enough to set the hook. I have tried many rods over the years and this set-up produces fish. So as soon as these guys approached my boat I start in with the old, "Guys, don't worry about rods... you don't need those rods. I have stuff all set up for you. Just, please, put them back in your cars."

Well, they simply would not hear of it. They were using their own rods, case closed. As they handed the rods to me to put on the boat, I thought they might have been joking. Someone had put them up to this. Each pole was between thirty and fifty years old and they were not bass rods either. They were generic party boat rods. These rods one found in the corner of a garage sale for 2 dollars. It looked like the line had never been changed. One pole looked like it deserved to be retired and hung over a fireplace in a lodge somewhere. When I asked why they insisted on using them, they told me that they were their fathers' and grandfathers' rods and they preferred to use them.

I still did not get it. In examining the rods closer I protested: "But they are not firm enough to handle the weight...and this one is missing two eyes and the drag doesn't even work on this one here!"

"Captain," said the guy who put the trip together, "These are the rods we are using."

What could I say? We'd be lucky to land anything with these rods. To me the idea of coming back to the dock without a big fish that people could oooh and ahhh over was maddening. Nevertheless, I put leaders on the rods and off we went. The whole way out I lectured the silent group about the importance of good equipment. Well, as it turns out, fishing was red hot and at one point all four guys hooked up. They were all very quiet, no yelling or laughing. All I heard was those old reels laboring as huge stripers screamed off line. I was sure they would explode. The guy whose reel had no drag was pulling line off manually. Rods were bent in half with fish. I was sure they would break, but somehow we got all the fish in. Three of the stripers were over forty pounds. One was real close to fifty and the guy decided to throw it back. I was amazed. I guess the grandfathers were looking down. What a cool thing to have witnessed. This was fishing at its best.

Even though I was making some money chartering and selling my two fish limit on the side to my catering friend in Sag Harbor, I still was spending too much money fishing by myself in pursuit of a trophy. There were so many striped bass around between 2006 and 2010 anyone could go out on a good tide and catch ten bass. I could have easily made a grand or more a night. A guy in Westhampton said he would take every fish I had. Even though I was a now a marked man by Maffaro and the boys, I knew that the odds of my getting caught were still very small. Joey Boy was the best at what he did, no doubt, but he simply had too much territory to cover, essentially all of Suffolk County. According to an article by Monte Burke in *Forbes* magazine, all of Long Island only had a handful of D.E.C officers to cover well over one-hundred miles of shore line.

I describe myself as a poacher and bootlegger of striped bass in the loosest sense of the word. Truth be told, I am exaggerating a bit as I am not a poacher. The definition of a poacher according to Wikipedia is "the illegal taking of wild plants or animals". While I have always been a bit of a scofflaw, taking a bunch of fish over my limit is simply is not in my nature. My conscious will not allow it. In ten years of fishing Montauk, I have had hundreds of people on my boat; none of them will say that they have seen me take over my limit of fish, because it never happened. Personally I believe in karma.

If I needed money that badly I would borrow from someone. I would take my chances at robbing a convenience store before I came in the inlet with a bunch of striped bass to sell. Also, ever since the Andy incident I was a marked man. My marina had cameras everywhere, and the D.E.C could seize them any time. And many fishermen and locals, probably trying to work a deal with the D.E.C themselves, were dying to blow the whistle on me.

What I was, and at first I didn't realize it, was a bootlegger. That is, I illegally sold fish to restaurants, an activity that was not illegal years ago and practiced by just about everyone. Now compared to the vast multi-million dollar criminal operation that was busted in Virginia and Maryland a couple of winters ago, I was a joke. Nevertheless I was a bootlegger by definition as I sold striped bass illegally without a license. What makes this, seemingly benign activity, bad, is it takes money directly out of the hands of authorized licensed commercial fisherman as they try to make a living. It does this by driving down the demand for their fish and subsequently the price they get paid for their catch.

My operation was this: I would leave the dock around six pm to catch the dusk bite (often I was alone, if I was not I would take my friends for free and they would leave their fish with me to sell in- stead of gas money). If I got a slob right off, I would keep her. This happened a few times and would generally be the biggest fish of the night. Now in the spirit of complete candor I must say if I happened across a much bigger fish during the course of the night, say forty five pounds and up, I would keep her for ego's sake. This was indeed breaking the law. I would then throw my other big fish to another boat or cut the smaller fish up on deck. This happened probably three times in ten years. Certainly, a weak moral move on my part. Still I sleep at night knowing that I spent a lot of time with fish pulling water over their gills and making sure they were revitalized in good shape to swim off. Often times I would spend 10 minutes with a fish, before it gave the signature shake of her tale indicating that it was ready to swim off. I hope those fish made it.

Most of the time, I did catch and release, having fun picking through the thirty to forty pound bass hoping for the slob. Again this was the golden age of bass fishing. It is hard to believe the seventies, or any other time in history had this many big fish this thick. Some evenings I would have fifteen to twenty fish all over thirty pounds. Toward the end of the night, around 10:30 or so, I would look to keep a fish under forty inches and by midnight take one over forty inches (my legal limit). I would go back to the dock clean the fish put the fillets in plastic zip lock bags and store them in my cooler in my van or truck. Then I went to sleep in my cabin or van, setting my alarm for 4 am when I went out caught the first-light bight. I would do this for three days straight. On the fourth morning I would not fish if I had a 48-inch Igloo cooler crammed with striper fillets. It was time to go to market.

The oldest fish in my cooler was three days old, still far fresher than any fish you will order at a restaurant or find at a fish market in New York City. So I had a product that restaurants wanted and had value. Then I would drive into Manhattan, sell the fish, and then go to my mom's old rent controlled apartment on Park Avenue and sleep for three days straight. I always kept one or two fellies for my 85 year old Korean neighbor. If I was unable to sell all the fish, I would give it to a local Fire Station; they always loved it, as fire- men, unlike cops, have a lot of free time on their hands and inside the station they have kitchens. One station I gave fish two lost men on 9/11. My friend told me I should sell to Fire Stations. There was no way I was doing that; it felt good giving it away.(By the way, people like when you give them striped bass, but go give them tuna and they are *indebted* too you)

One day a chef in Westhampton Beach wanted four whole fish and would pay me four dollars a pound, a decent price at the time. I had no car so I called a cab. With the help of the Pink Tuna cab driver we barely got the cooler that weighed well over one hundred pounds into the trunk. He dropped me off at the train station, where it took me a good half hour to drag the fish laden cooler up the ramp, inch by inch, foot by foot. I took the train to Westhampton where the buyer, a Portuguese chef met me at the station. By the way, Portuguese will always buy but beware; they are shrewd. We took the fish out of my cooler and put them into another cooler in the back of his van, cash was exchanged and he drove off. Then I waited with my empty cooler for the eastbound train. It was all quite fun and exciting.

I never sold in Montauk; the restaurants in town bought only from the fish houses at a fair price, there was such an abundance of fresh fish sold directly from the whole sale fish houses legally, the Montauk restaurant's had no reason to break the law. Sometimes I would hit the Japanese and Chinese joints in East Hampton. They gave me cash but never put the fish on the menu. They simply ate it themselves. All Spanish restaurants take the fish but will never give you cash. Rather they will give you a food credit. Say three meals for one smaller fish. They always want the whole fish, not fillets. The tony New York City restaurants were the fun ones to sell to. I sold to them all, mostly SoHo and the meat market area in Chelsea around Fourteenth Street. At the time the gas prices were not that bad and I would drive all the way to Manhattan after four nights of fishing. I had to wait to mid-July when the warm water had driven the fish away from the Western Sound and Raritan Bay. In June poachers and bootleggers from Jersey and Nassau County inundate the restaurants with fish. The Manhattan restaurants freeze the fish as they can't buy or sell striped bass legally until July 1. But by mid-July they are running low and local fisherman cannot catch fish, as the fish have moved east into cooler waters... that's when I rolled into town.

Truth be told, I think I was becoming more addicted to the thrill and adrenalin rush of selling the fish, than catching the fish in the first place. I with my little cooler of fish was right there in all the action. Like a merchant in the ancient Kasbah, this was commerce! I was a player. I was moving goods and merchandise, so to speak. Sometimes you had to wait for the head chef or owner to write you a check or bring you cash. On a Friday the places were bustling, with two or three prep chefs chopping up various vegetables or trimming some type of beef and trucks constantly pulling up with deliveries. In one awkward moment a chef was weighing my fish on a scale as the fish delivery guy came in to drop his order of swordfish, salmon and scallops. Striped bass was conspicuously absent from his order form and box. He did not say anything, but he looked at the scale and then at me; he knew exactly what was going on. This is how striped bass was sold; this is how it was done.

I knew an out of work construction worker who decided in 2008 to make a living illegally selling bass. It became his full time job. He lived on the South Shore of Long Island, and was coming through Jones inlet loaded down with fish every day. With no fear of the law, he would throw the fish into the back of his Jeep, and drive them into Manhattan, and sell them to East Village restaurants. Though he was a friend, I made several appeals to him to go easier on the fish, trying in vain to make clear to him that it was not an infinite resource. He did this night in and night out and bragged about how much he was making. I remember thinking that he was a dirt bag. Turning him in would probably have earned me some leniency in the impending Andy court case, but at the time it was not in my nature.

Maybe the reader is thinking at this point what's the difference, it just semantics between what my friend was doing and what I was doing. We were both filthy poachers. While I could see why one may think this, bare me out, the difference (and there is one) is bored out in simple math. Assuming I am telling the truth, I fished five full moon nights and took two fish. This equals ten fish taken from the fishery over five nights. My friend would take ten fish a night, or more, in five nights. That equals fifty+ fish taken, compared to my ten in five days.

Caught

Up and down the east coast there are fisherman who see striped bass only as a dollar sign. I saw keeping my legal limit as a way to pay for my gas bill, so I could continue my addiction.

*

The Decline

Fishing Addiction: the Consequences

Not willing to make money as a blatant poacher, and depressed over my friend's greed and lack of respect for stripers. I found a day job as a part-time gym attendant at Gurney's Inn in Montauk. The gym supervisor soon was set on firing me, and she was very confident about her argument. I must be let go, she said, because I often came to work smelling like fish. As I had been warned several times to "smell better," there was nothing that anyone could say to refute her. When any rebuttal arose on my behalf, she would dismiss it by saying, "Yes, but he smells like fish and we are trying to run a high-end health spa."

Another woman, I was told, came to my defense. "Look," she contended, "customers like Jeff. Sure he's a little quirky, but he is usually on time, he is honest and he helps people when they don't know how to use the equipment." To which the supervisor nodded and, enunciating slowly as if speaking to a bunch of first graders, said "Despite several warnings, he... still... SMELLS... LIKE... FISH." There is no beating this argument. In the end, no matter how good a worker is or how well liked he may be, if the guy smells like fish, nothing is going to help him.

No amount of showering will get night after night of catching and cleaning striped bass off your body. But in my experience that odor can signal a larger problem: the guy could be a fishing addict. From twenty years of hanging out at marinas it is my opinion that, short of infidelity, fishing addiction has destroyed more marriages, jobs and friendships than anything else, including golf, which, while time consuming, can't hold a candle to true fishing addiction. Now at this point the reader might be thinking *fishing addiction?* But don't scoff. While fishing addiction may not have the terminal component of traditional addiction, having tangled with substance abuse years ago I can say that a lot of the fallout is the same: estrangement from family, lies, mania, financial ruin, etc.

While there are fewer of us out there, at this very moment there is some guy who showed up late to work today, having not had any substantial sleep in three days. He is looking at himself in the men's bathroom mirror: unshaven, conspicuous circles under eyes, sun burnt (not like the "oh you got too much sun at the beach, Bob," but the type of sunburn only a hobo can sport. You know it when you see it.) As the man desperately washes his hands trying to get the stench of fish off, a futile effort as I've mentioned, he thinks to himself *How could this have happened again? How could I have done this to myself again? To my loved ones?*

His colleagues are talking about him; they don't make eye contact with him. While he sits at his desk trying to focus and look productive, he is trying too hard, he is making no sense. Wiped out by noon, unable to keep his eyes open, the man takes a nap in his car. When he returns to the office at 3 pm, he is called into his boss' office and fired. This scenario happens. People say that fishing addiction is not as bad as drug addiction? Well, a lot of the results are the same: bankruptcy, estrangement from friends and family, divorce.

*

The Full Moon Beckons Like a Crack Pipe

I was obsessed with striped bass fishing. One time I was with my girlfriend Kara on vacation in the Greek Isles. We were having a great time, but then one night the full moon popped out from behind the clouds. For whatever reason, it looked especially big over there. Now, I booked the vacation knowing it was on a full moon, and that fishing would therefore be great in Montauk. But I guessed that I would be so far away, and having so much fun, I would not even think about the moon. I guess maybe I thought that there would not be a full moon when I was in Greece – perhaps they had different moon phases? But when I saw that huge moon come out, it began to call to me. All I could think about was striped bass fishing. Sadly, there is no sports fishing to speak of in the Mediterranean anymore; its waters have been picked clean by over fishing, and ravaged by dynamite. Talk about un-sportsman-like! We went skin diving in various places and there was not a minnow to be found. The fish stores on the Greek Isles are largely empty or sell imported tilapia.

When we went on vacation I had not yet cracked the coveted fifty-pound mark, and it was wearing on me. I had one at forty-nine pounds, and I had had some cows get off my hook. I simply had to go get my "fish on." Each night the moon grew bigger and my obsession worsened. Kara had a job in Athens the next day and I was going to stay one more night with her. But I simply had to catch the last night of the moon tide for a shot at a fifty-pounder. Once we hit Athens I told Kara (who could tell right away that once the moon popped up I was a goner) that I wanted to change my flight for a day earlier. Kara is an understanding woman, but this was beyond her grasp. It cost me a couple of hundred bucks to bump up the fight, but sure enough, I was on a flight to JFK the next day.

Once I landed I took the shuttle to Jamaica, Queens, where I just missed a train to Montauk. Finally, two hours later, I caught another train for the three-hour ride. I took a cab to the docks, where I met my friend Rick. We went out at 1 am. We caught a few fish, but nothing big; I was so fucking tired and cold, I remember wondering why I had done it. All bass fishermen romanticize. We remember that incredible force with which a big fish hits and the excitement, the adrenalin, when in reality a lot of bass fishing is tedious and fucking boring. It involves sitting there waiting, drift after drift, often in inhospitable weather, just to get the fish to feed. If you want to consistently catch big fish, get ready to be tired all the time. You must be able to fish tired; forget about a good night's sleep.

I have not failed to fish a full or a new moon in ten years. There is nothing like it. The beauty hits you at your spiritual core. I get choked up by simply thinking about how many wonderful nights I had on Block Island Sound the sunsets and the sunrises; I was blessed for sure.

In January, I'll wake up in the middle of the night wondering what had gone wrong with the big fish I lost last July. I will play over and over in my mind what I could have done differently. Why did I not change that frayed leader, or sharpen or change the hook, or tie a better knot? Then I start thinking about the next season, when the tide will start running at Block Island on the June full moon. What kind of bait should

I use? Live bunker? Perhaps anchor up and use bunker chunks, porgy chunks or mackerel... will frozen Mackerel work? This is the stuff I thought about constantly.

All I could think about was fish and fishing. My enthusiasm was obviously contagious as the phone was ringing with new charters from people who wanted to take me up on the "40-pound guarantee." They were calling about my ad in magazines and my videos on YouTube where I showed a ten-year-old boy reeling in a forty-seven pound bass. People who had never caught a forty-pounder wanted to fish with me at the "Pig Pen," and when I told them I was booked and they should call another charter boat, they would protest that they wanted to fish with me and only me. I was doing okay considering this is was time when people were not fishing as much. Most charter boats in Montauk are great but I guess some go through the motions. Sure my boat was sloppy and plain, but everyone who hired me got a trophy.

Customers often left me with extra fish or fillets. I also went out on my own a lot. I did not have to go far. I could catch my two fish limit right at Shagwong Point, a half a mile from the harbor. I had two restaurants in South Hampton willing to buy my extra fish, and if they were not interested, I could always find someone who was. Never underestimate the selling power of fresh (as in swimming the day before) fish; restaurants need it, even if Joey and the boys are lurking about.

One time I took out a guy who was a true sportsman and a gentleman. The fishing was great and he had already landed a fish above forty pounds that he was keeping to eat. The other fish were going back to live another day. Then he pulled in a fish that was close to fifty inches with a nice fat belly, bigger than his keeper. Excited by bragging rights back at the docks, I grabbed it by the lips and held it up for him. "You're going to keep her right?!" I barked. The man shook his head, "I have already got my limit and I don't need the meat."

"Yes," I replied, "but this is a trophy, you could mount this one and put it over your fireplace. It is a fifty-pounder for sure! I will say I caught the smaller one." Reluctantly the guy agreed, but I could tell that he was disgusted or at least taken back with my greed and ego. At the dock the fish fell just south of the coveted fifty-pounds (49.50). While he had a great day and we did release a lot of fish, I could tell that he was upset that he killed this old breeder. We took some pictures and gave the fish to the dock attendant. (With the PCb's counts in those big fish I hope the guy didn't feed it to his children.)

As with alcohol, as soon as I am driving down 27 East toward Montauk, I start to become anesthetized. My mind begins to race: where can I get the baitfish? Where will I do my first drift? Do I need new fuses? Will my line work well? Do I need to add new numbers to my GPS? Should I use a fluorocarbon leader or not? Some of this is a healthy distraction from life, but when people start putting fishing and the huge expense of it before friends and family responsibilities then it becomes problematic. Even extremely wealthy people have a tough time justifying fishing all the time. Countless weddings, graduations and funerals are missed due to fishing for striped bass, and it gets really sad when a child's college fund gets dipped into to pay the marina bill or to add a new GPS unit.

From Wikipedia:

"Classic hallmarks of addiction include: impaired control over substances/behavior, preoccupation with substance/behavior, continued use despite consequences, and denial."

Caught

One time I sold a 1998 Subaru Outback with only fifty thousand miles on the odometer for $2800 to pay my marina bill. (In my defense the car did smell like fish, and I thought it might be impossible to get rid of the odor.) However, while embarrassing and pathetic, this is not the saddest example of the depths to which I sank in the scramble for funds to feed my addiction. My mother had given me a signed first edition set of Rudyard Kipling that had been in my family for generations and told me that if I ever found myself in desperate need of cash I could probably get a nice price for them. I had them on the shelf for years and never even looked at them. I was under the impression that Kipling was an imperialist and a racist; that educating the world was the "white man's burden." Granted he wrote in a vastly different time, but I was slightly embarrassed to even have the collection. Still I never considered selling them.

Until, that is, I heard about an approaching striped bass tournament with a five hundred dollar entry fee and a $5,000 first prize (including side bets called calcuttas). Time to sell the books. I took one of the volumes into a high end store in Manhattan on Fifth Avenue, and the people there said that they were indeed interested as they had just sold the same set for eight thousand dollars. They tempered the news with, "Of course, we could not give you that amount, but if they were in good shape we might be interested." At the same time, I was in contact via email with a guy from webuyrarebooks4cash.com and made an appointment with him the next day. When I brought the signed edition of *The Jungle,* down to the high-end bookstore, the guy I spoke to before was not there. A very pleasant British woman at the counter told me that, while they were in the market for such a collection, the first volume, the signed one, was in pretty bad shape and needed about five hundred dollars of spine work. She told me she was not sure if the decision maker, who she was not, would be interested but asked me to leave the book there for a few days. A few days! The tournament was in two days! The long and the short of it was that I took nineteen hundred bucks from the webuyrarebooks4cash guy to pay off my marina bill, buy some floral carbon leader and enter a stupid tournament (which I lost by 1/10th of a pound!) I still feel sick to my stomach writing this down. Even though those books were never cracked open, I yearn to have them back. They have taken on a mythical air to me. I stare at an empty shelf and envision having Norman Rockwell-ish "Kipling parties" on a cold winter night in a well-lit room tucked into a nice brownstone in Manhattan with my friends and family all around.

I am not sure why I am babbling on about books to illustrate fishing addiction. My present living condition is the most vivid and concrete example I have: I live in a van. Let me repeat that: I live in a van. A blue Chevy 1995 conversion van. That's what happens when you plan your life around moon fazes, you end up living in a fucking van.

Worse than the rare book story is how I ended up in the van. My family had a three bedroom rent stabilized apartment on 82 and Park Avenue, 2 blocks from the Metropolitan Museum of Art and Central Park. My mom had set up two meetings with a lawyer to see if she could transfer the lease to my name. I was a no show on both dates as they fell on the September full moon. The lease expired. So long Park Ave. Hello van. This would be actually funny if I was a younger man. I am 47 fucking years old! Fishing addiction. Has become very real to me and it ain't so funny.

During my heavy drinking days (about 1988 in college), each time before my first drink, before my conscience was numbed by booze, I was a bundle of nerves. I was consumed with issues that all undergrads rightly should worry about: financial aid payments, upcoming final exams and papers due, returning parent's calls, etc. and keenly aware that getting drunk and stoned on a Tuesday afternoon was clearly not the best choice. But once that first Pabst Blue Ribbon (PBR) hit my blood stream all worries, and I mean all worries, simply fell away like a woman's robe in a James Bond movie.

*

An Epiphany

It became the same for me with fishing. It was so hard to justify the cost of it all, the gas and subsequent environmental impact, the time away from home, the equipment, even the price of bait, which has doubled in five years. I mean here I was a smelly forty-two-year-old man drifting round Block Island Sound with no real career or family. One time I was out there all by myself on the fourth of July feeling lonely and sad that I was not at the any of the wonderful fireworks displays that I saw up and down the Connecticut and Rhode Island coast line, but once a big fish hit, the "wack," and the line went tight and screamed off, all trepidation fell away. I did not feel alone. All was right with the world in my view. I submit that when one has a big fish on, loneliness doesn't exist.

Neither did my ADD. For the next five minutes I was hyper focused on getting that fish in the boat. Then it was off to the market place with the fish. That is to "bootleg," to knock on the back doors of Manhattan restaurants and get ready to barter. This was as exciting for me as catching the fish; I felt like a player. It was as though I was a character in *Goodfellas*. One day I had an epiphany, I remember racing to a restaurant with a cooler full of fresh cut fillets and thinking, "What am I doing?" I had crossed the line from fishing enthusiast to someone who only saw a fish as a dollar sign.

I was also moved by a public service ad meant to deter people from training pit bulls to fight and making money on them a la Michael Vick. Certainly a despicable pastime by any standard and, I told myself, certainly not an accurate metaphor for what I was up to. I mean I was just selling a couple of fish, but still the ad resonated with me. It had a picture of a sweet-looking pit bull looking up and a caption bubble coming out of its mouth, "Why do you have to make money off of me...get a job loser." The reality was that I was making money off a fish that was in trouble, a fish that was always good to me, a fish that had given me tremendous joy and pleasure for many years. Was everyone doing it? Yes! Was I taking more than my two fish limit? No... But that was the problem; too many guys were and have been poaching bass. It needed to stop. If you want self-esteem you need to do estimable things, I am told. Illegally selling fish out of the trunk of my car did not exactly fit under the umbrella of estimable acts.

Even though I was willing to cut out selling fish, I still wanted to catch a giant striper over sixty pounds. With all these hours logged in I was starting to get very proficient at catching big stripers. I knew when and where they would be, and the most likely time they would chew, and I was there. It was only a matter of time before I crossed paths with a sixty pounder. And this time I had the correct knots and hooks.

*

Big Fish Little Dick: The Last of the Trophy Hunters

Trophy fishing is so engrained in me, I would be lying if I did not admit to still having a smidgen of pride at all the big fish I brought to the dock. I've taken probably fifty fish over forty pounds with a few forty-nine pounders and three over fifty. But mostly I am genuinely disappointed and embarrassed by my ego, that I was so obsessed with dragging fish around the marina and showing them off. Rather, I should have taken a picture and let the big female breeders, the top of their species, go free. When it comes to killing big fish I'm schizophrenic. The dichotomy; it is like a light switch. I can be walking down the block at my present job as a dog walker in Manhattan and be smiling at the memory of weighing in giant fish I caught. I'll be absolutely proud and beaming thinking about the fish I killed, then the next minute full of remorse and sorrow at my destruction of the wonderful fish. Really one of the only reasons I wrote this book was to prevent me from slaughtering fish for another season. I mean how could I sell fish or weigh in a trophy after this self-incriminating tell-all? Having said this, I will surely miss the lifestyle.

These days catching and killing a fish and weighing it in for vanity's sake is looked upon with almost the same disgust as shooting a mountain lion and having its head mounted above a fireplace. That is, people just don't do it anymore. Most fishermen now don't like "trophy hunters." My own understanding of the importance of letting big fish go took a while to take hold. It is a process for everyone.

The only good news and the reason I can sleep at night, is that truth be told I am not the best angler in the word. I dropped a lot of big fish over the years. I would say at least fifty-percent of big fish that I had on the line got away twenty seconds into the fight. A lot of fish would scream out twenty feet of line like a raped ape and spit the hook. For years I used generic dull hooks that could not break your skin. I can think of at least twenty individual times that really big fish got off unharmed. As a trophy hunter I was tortured by these experiences. I would repeat what happened over and over again in my head. I would lie awake at night thinking about it months later. Was I using too thin a line? Was my drag too tight? Did I check my leader? Did I check the top of my leader? Was there a nick or cut in the line? Why didn't I change the line or cut it back or use a better swivel? But now I am glad they got away to live another day, unharmed after a short fight. Hallelujah!

I loved weighing in big fish so much I would go to any length to justify killing them. I would say that big fish, the apex predators (which they are), devoured all the small fish and that they were the reason there were no flounder and lobster around anymore (this is actually a fair point.) I would say that the average fifty-pound bass was going to probably die that year anyway. The justification went on and on.

During this time, however, something else was at work: I was getting more and more disappointed by the fight some of these huge fish were giving me. I was beginning to realize that a thirty-six pound striped bass fought harder than a fifty-pounder just about every time. In my bass-ing career, I landed five fish around the fifty-pound mark and only one gave me a reasonable fight. I have had some thirty-pound fish on the line that I swore were sixty-pounders. A forty-pounder will scream out line, but the fifty pounders always seemed to swim to the surface. Slowly my insatiable desire to catch and weigh in big fish began to subside. I also knew that it would be impossible to have a family or even a relationship fishing the way I was. It simply demanded too many hours. And the Andy court case was constantly on my mind. I was now getting weekly calls from Maffaro asking me what I was going to do. I was also noticing that more and more fish were coming up with red dots or lesions on them.

As outrageous as it sounds, the group that I am most sympathetic to, when it comes to the annihilation of the striped bass, is the "trophy hunters" who abide by fishing regulations. After all, going out and "catching the big one" is part of the very fabric of sport fishing. If we demonize the thrill of landing a big fish, killing it, weighing it, and showing it off at the dock to friends, are we not tampering with the fundamental pastime of sport fishing as we know it? I still have a picture of me at around ten-years-old with the Judge proudly displaying a huge trophy trout. We are both grinning from ear to ear. From an early age trophy fishing has been injected into my blood stream.

Before we burn the trophy hunter at the stake, like so many want to do, let's examine the culture in which he was raised. Big fish were always romanticized and sought. Ernest Hemingway made sport fishing cool with the wonderful black and white photographs of him standing with giant blue marlins and large tuna he captured off of Cuba and Key West Florida. Didn't many fireplaces (and some still do) sport proudly above their mantels a variety of mounted trophy fish? My parents' home had a six-and-a-half-pound brown trout that I caught when I was 11, ice fishing on a pound. How about the wealthy CEOs; don't they often have mounted fish on their walls? Many of the fishing groups that are now protesting the killing of big bass have trophy mounts in their clubhouses. Many fishing magazines send mixed messages. While their articles all seem to stress the importance of catch-and-release some sponsor "heaviest fish contests" and have trophy pages. From an early age, trophy fishing was ingrained in me and many others.

It is tough not to smile at the immense and distorted egos of the trophy Striped bass fisherman who fish by boat with live bait. One night I raised on the VHF radio a good friend of mine to see if he was catching at a certain spot. He came back with this reply: "Yeah, I got them to chew over here." Let me repeat: he got them (the fish) "to chew." He did not say, "Yes, we are catching over here," or "Yes, the fish are chewing over here," or "Yes, the bite is on - thank god!" No, he got them "to chew", as if it had nothing to do with the live eel he used for bait – that he violently impaled on the hook; the eel never gets any credit. Yes, my friend should get some credit for reading the tide chart correctly and presenting the bait well, I suppose. But I am more impressed with the fly guy or surf fisherman who make their own lures, or the captain I profile in this book who fashioned his own lure by pounding out sheet metal by hand in his garage one cold winter.

The fact of the matter, and the very point of this book, is that no matter how good an angler is, no matter how prepared he is, *if da fish ain't a dere, you ain't a cathin' no fish!*

Sport fishing is a billion-dollar industry creating many jobs. Where would it be if trophy fishing were outlawed? In the past ignorance certainly was bliss. The pursuit of giant fish was once something to be proud of. It was a part of American culture along with baseball and apple pie. However, now, the "inconvenient truth" is that striped bass trophy fishermen should leave the big breeding females (forty-pounds plus) alone. They are necessary for the survival of the species. Not only do they produce huge "mother lode" amounts of fertile eggs they are also older fish or "survivors" with good genes. Perhaps more savvy to the traps of men, able to skillfully navigate around polluted waterways and gillnets that are legally and illegally littering the east coast shores at this moment. As most big fish over fifty pounds swim alone, away from the school many of these cows are not infected with bacterial disease.

As for the contention that stripers aren't tasty when they are old, I don't think that's the case. I don't think striped bass taste that good when they are small either. They are a meaty fish. This writer is partial to a whiter fish like porgies, blackfish, flounder, fluke or my favorite sea bass. As I stated earlier, the older bass, the "slobs" or "cows" contain more PCBs than smaller fish, and should not be eaten. Once a year, these fish migrate up rivers to spawn, like the Hudson, where General Electric admittedly dumped huge amounts of metal containing PCBs. A forty-pound fish would have entered the Hudson and been exposed repeatedly.

Usually when I am cleaning fish for a customer and they ask about the mercury and PCBs in bass and whether or not they are safe to eat, I look at them and say, "Listen, I've been eating this stuff for years and I am doing great." They give me a once over, then say something along the lines of, "Well you know, we had a lot of fun just catching them. You can keep our fish. Thanks."

I am old school. I like to catch the fish, kill it, put it on ice, weigh it in at the marina's official scale, take pictures and then give it to the dock boys or sell it to a restaurant. I will occasionally barter with the restaurant for a fifty-dollar food credit or something. Point is I like the whole process. I like icing the boat down, I like the blood and guts, I like installing a new GPS, I like painting the bottom of the boat every year. I had a friend entertaining the idea of buying a boat. I warned him what a headache and responsibility it is to own a boat. Then I asked him what I ask a lot of people who entertain the idea of getting a boat: what do you like about fishing?

This is kind of a trick question because the only real answer has to be: everything. The guys that give a general answer like: "I just like to get a few friends together and enjoy the outdoors" in my experience don't last no matter how rich they are. Even a Donald Trump doesn't want to get hit with a sixty thousand dollar marina bill when he only uses a boat five times. Of course, he has the money but it just does not make sense to spend it this way. You've got to love it all, the good weather and the bad weather, endless amounts of time listening to the forecast, looking at tide charts, for three hours straight cleaning the boat, then cleaning the fish at the cleaning table and packing out the fish. You've got to love tying hooks, trouble-shooting, coming to terms with the fact that everything breaks and corrodes. Realizing that every day is not Christmas when it comes to fishing and sometimes they just don't bite. And perhaps most importantly, realizing that all of the people that you thought would want to go fishing with you, never come, or only come once.

Fishing is not a part of American culture the way it once was. And this is not just because the middle class has no money anymore, I have sadly seen my share of dumbfounded rich guys begging me to fish with them just so they are not alone. They are not bad guys and they have loads of friends at home, but most people just don't hold up on the water. Either they get seasick or there are other things they would rather be doing, like watching television or playing with their newest gadget. Their kids have no interest in fishing in most cases. Eventually, the guy who bought the boat will stop using it. The next year it is up for sale. Some friendly advice: if the reason you are buying a boat is that your "friends" will come fishing with you, then don't because they won't!

I have seen my share of friendships get destroyed over fishing. Now more than ever, just because everything is so fucking expensive. Sport fishing, for everyone, is very tough to justify.

*

Partnerships - Some Advice

And never, ever, ever split a boat with someone. In the history of boating "partnering" has never worked out! I would be a particularly bad partner, sloppy and not handy. No one talks about it but years ago Christopher Columbus used to have a partner but the guy was always busy with his family or golfing and never used the boat, and Chris always had the thing out. Anyway, at the end of the season they still split the marina and maintenance bill down the middle. Well, the friend tried to reason with Christopher, "Look Chris, I like you and all and respect what you are doing...but man... I used the boat, what two, three times this year and they were all local short Mediterranean trips. You took the boat all over the fucking world; you should pay for most of these bills."

But Christopher replied, "Look, the boat needs work, we both own it. A deal is a deal. I can't help if your kids hate the boat and your wife gets seasick and is a whiny skank. Now pay up!" Well, like so many others, they ended up in small claims court.

*

Career Choice Revisited

I visited Harwichport last winter - the place where I was bitten with the fishing bug as a child. Like I mentioned earlier the public docks were cleaner but lacked much of the character I remembered. I mean this seriously, not in a nostalgic way like, "Man, Times Square in Manhattan was so much better in the seventies with the peep shows and the hookers and purse snatchers." The place I revisited had an almost vulgar, utilitarian feel to it: a cement pier, a very clean, barren parking lot, a boat ramp and only a couple of boats, no charter boats and only one commercial boat at the end of the pier.

It staggers me to think how such a wholesome and wonderful childhood fishing experience could degenerate into this essay I wrote in an email to myself. I guess I felt that my situation was becoming atypical and I should document it.

"I just got back from Montauk and had to walk by all the kids and parents going to PS 6 again. They looked so happily civilized and domestic. It really felt like the days I had coming home after staying up all night doing coke. I reeked of fish; they looked at me like a homeless guy...This is so uncivilized; in Montauk I stayed up two nights in a row with basically no sleep. The short nap I had in my wet, freezing sleeping bag was tempered by a nightmare. Nothing ensures weird creepy dreams like sleeping in a small, dank cabin with a wet, cold sleeping bag that smells like rotten fish (in the most real way imaginable) and using a propped-up life ring and tackle box as a pillows. It was cold, in the high thirties both nights. The zipper on my damp sleeping bag was broken so I could not retain body heat. I was also getting up periodically dumping buckets of water into a trashcan I had placed on my deck in an effort to keep the bait alive for the next morning's tournament. (I did not have an aerated live well for the bait.) My feet were cramping due to the cold, and so at one point I got up and ran down the dock in an effort to increase circulation. That night as I lay there the only thing that gave me the slightest bit of solace was the idea that I was getting a taste, JUST a taste, of what the good people

who fought in the Revolutionary and Civil Wars must have gone through in the middle of the winter. But they were fighting for what they believed in, for the most part, while I am simply a fishing junkie, a fool, an addict. They were fighting for a cause while I was fighting for bragging rights, to catch the biggest fish in the harbor, and walk around swinging my dick around. As it turns out I did not catch anything all day, so I stayed out for the night tides. So that is a total of twenty hours. I pulled into the harbor at daybreak as the fleet of morning charter boats were pulling out, full of buoyant, happy customers. I was exhausted and in pain. Early on in the night I had kicked the spine of a bass and it had gone through my sneaker and punctured my skin. Not a big problem necessarily, but I had never done that before and I had heard of terrible infections occurring from this type of accident. This thought was occupying space in my mind. The problem was that I had spent plenty of money on gas and bait in the last few days, and had nothing to show for it except that I had found some good places that I recorded with my GPS. Those places held big, possibly tournament-winning fish and there was a tournament coming in the a.m. that I was poised to place well in.

I also had two striped bass that I could sell for a hundred bucks if I could only find a customer. I knew we could not have them on the boat when we left the harbor. So I put them in my buddy's cooler on his boat. I had the self-esteem of a street hooker, or probably worse because I had not generated any income. The day before, the guys who said they were going to come on "my charter" never showed up, so rather than exhibit discipline and stay at the dock, I basically went on a two hundred dollar joy ride to Block Island. The weather got worse and I took a real beating on the way back across Block Island Sound. The wind was against the tide the whole way back, and the unyielding waves knocked out my GPS, depth finder and lights. My lower back and kidneys were killing me and my toe was throbbing. A two hundred dollar self-indulgent trip! I had caught my limit of fish, but I had no one lined up to sell them to. I felt like garbage and the boat was a complete mess. I smelled like fish. At the dock, I was so ashamed I did not want to make eye contact with other fisherman or the owners of the marina. I felt like I had been doing coke all night as the sun rose. Same exact feeling. When I returned to the dock, as was always the case, I would see clean, well-dressed families looking forward to a day of sports fishing. I wished them luck – I know how much fun can be had on a boat with friends – but now I was a 42-year-old degenerate. I knew once the tournament was over, that once I got the boat cleaned up and I had gotten some sleep I would be fine. I would ride the Hampton Jitney to Manhattan and take twenty pound of fillets I had acquired over three days down to Chinatown and try to unload them for two hundred bucks. But that would not be easy because Chinatown is not willing to take risks like they used too. They all want "tagged fish." After the tournament I got on the bus Manhattan. I had tried to wash my clothes, to no avail. The guy next to me knew I was the source of the rank smell that contaminated the entire bus. His disgust was palpable. I have got to stop fishing this way. But I know after a couple of days rest the monster will be back, and I will find a way to get back on the rips."

This captures only what I felt like on that night and the next day. It does not mention the exhilaration I felt landing huge striped bass and the high I got from weighing in the biggest fish in the marina. Nor does it go into the physical toll. I used to fish all day and most of the night, get back to the marina at 2 am, get in my car and drive, or, as I used to jest, "time travel" all the way back to Manhattan. It is well known that driving exhausted is as dangerous as driving while intoxicated. Before I started using the bus, a few times when my eyes grew heavy, I pulled over and slept. Other times, when I had to work I couldn't. It wasn't an option.

Because the fishing is so repetitive – finding the fish, drifting over the fish, presenting them with bait, hooking up or missing fish, then running back up again to do the same thing over again – your body takes a toll for sure. I have been pretty crippled after five days and nights fishing. God only knows what the long-term effects will be. Not only to my spine, but to my internal organs. Also, my diet really began to suck. I would eat whatever I could lay my hands on, or whatever junk food was around. Sometimes I would not eat at all. I never drank alcohol out on the ocean, but the next day I felt hung-over, the emotional high always followed by a melancholy depression.

One last, small anecdote could summarize my attitude to fishing. I was talking with a guy at the docks once, a responsible guy with two kids, a wife and a house, yada-yada. Well, we got to chatting about boats and he told me how he was all set to buy a nice second-hand thirty-foot fishing boat. He had made a down payment and everything. But, he then found out that, due to an erosion problem, he needed to put in a new driveway at his house. The guy smiled at me and shrugged his shoulders with an air of acceptance and said, resigned, "Well there goes the new boat." I looked at him like he should be committed to a mental ward; to me he was the crazy one. What? Invest in the upkeep of a legitimate capital asset instead of buying a boat that depreciates in value by fifty-percent the day you buy it and will cost fifteen thousand a year even if you do not use it? And will be eaten away by salt. Insane!

Once while fishing close to Block Island on a remarkably calm night, or a "real greaser" (as my friend Joe calls it), after a good hook set and a tremendous run-off, a giant fish came to the surface about twenty five yards away to our east. It was slashing about on top trying to throw the hook. It was so calm out we could hear the thunderous slashes the fish was making with her, no doubt immense, tail. That's what big fish often do. They go to the surface and try to rock back and forth to shake the hook. Keep the line tight and rod bent to prevent this from happening. In this case, the front of the boat was actually being pulled around by the fish due east toward the fish and Block Island. I had never witnessed this before. This was a heavy, heavy fish. We had already boated a forty-three pounder, that fought hard, but stayed down, and this seemed much bigger. Then, just like that, the line went slack and the fish was gone. I did not understand what could have happened with this new Gamakatsu hook (amazingly sharp, effective hooks.) The fish was on the surface away from rocks and boulders that could cut and sever the line. How did the line break? Did a bluefish come up and bight the sinker? I was using sixty-pound leaders and I was constantly checking for frays and nicks. I had lost fish due to nicks in the line before so I was always checking. When I reeled the line in I was horrified at what I saw - the worst thing any fisherman can see - a curlycue at the end of the leader and no hook! This could only mean one thing: the hook slipped because of a badly tied knot! This is the worst possible way to lose a fish. I screamed for ten minutes in a rage; you could have heard me on the Connecticut side. I was inconsolable, my fishing friend was bewildered by my rage (in fact he never came with me again, despite having a twenty fish night himself.) I was mad for weeks at my rookie mistake.

But now, years later I like to take some solace in thinking that this particular beast of a fish is still alive somewhere. She is hook-shy now, smarter, more discriminating when it comes to food and baits. She can use this knowledge to refuse the next eel or piece of bunker or lure that looks suspicious. Or if she does happen to get caught again (that lucky fisherman!), hopefully it's by a better man than I who will release the fish to live another day, to breed another season. This fish could very well still be alive I like to think.

*

Terry's Underwear

To me, nothing illustrates the power that striped bass can have over a person like the story of Terry Blackwell, a beloved music teacher and fisherman from Suffolk County, Long Island, who died when his boat flipped in rough seas. I interviewed several people who were at Terry's crowded funeral, including a fifty-two year old man named Jamie who thirty years earlier was on the boat the day Terry died. When I heard about the funeral ceremony, I could not help but draw parallels with the movie *Mr. Holland's Opus* starring Richard Dreyfuss. Former and current students of Terry's played instruments in perfect harmony at the funeral, both celebrating his short life and mourning his passing.

As passionate as Terry was about music and teaching, and as much as he loved his family and students, few could deny it was the lure of the striped bass that called him to his death, leaving Jamie to swim for shore in fifty degree water as Terry was swept helplessly out to sea by the outgoing tide. Only a striped bass fisherman can understand the hypnotic spell these fish can have over a person.

The striper addict fishes exhausted and works exhausted. Terry was committed to this life and for a few years it paid off. He was doing what he loved, teaching, fishing and making extra money on the side selling fish, which was legal in 1981. (It is amazing how many regulations there are today and how few existed then.) Fishing paid for his hobby and justified his being away night after night. Terry did not squander his earnings on drugs and alcohol, and his family benefited from the income.

Terry did not have the huge ego that most bass fishermen have. He was not desperate to be on the front covers of any fishing magazines. He was understated and soft spoken with a pleasant demeanor. Sure he liked to be respected by other fishermen; he had some hubris and liked to sheepishly nod his head and smile when people asked if "he got a big one" the night before - but he was not a blowhard. He was well liked at the marina.

Sadly, Terry's love for fishing was not as wholesome as one might think. Beneath the benign exterior of a sportsman, something more insidious had been fermenting. Plainly and simply, based on what I came up with talking with people at the docks, Terry had become addicted to the money.

It is important to stress again that he never broke any laws. Unlike today, it was not illegal to sell striped bass in the late 70's and early 80's, and you did not need a license or a permit. Anyone could sell any fish to whomever they wanted to. One could also catch as much fish as one wanted. There are many accounts of boats being so full of fish they were close to swamping. Terry was doing nothing wrong, simply making money. But not unlike the reality show *Dangerous Catch,* conditions were not always favorable off Montauk Point. At three dollars a pound, though, some guys would push the limit. Sure, the seas are not as treacherous as the Bering Sea in Alaska, but the boats are also smaller. Terry fished in a twenty-two-foot Boston Whaler.

Terry's addiction to fishing took a toll on his family as well. One source told me, "Terry spent more time in the parking lot of the marina with his cronies than with his family." That was a time when the "pin hookers" slept in trailers and pick-up trucks with covers over the bed. They were in every parking lot in Montauk. If you go to the marinas around Montauk today you'll see a camper here, a trailer there, but back in the late seventies, they were everywhere. Today the marina where Terry used to sleep doesn't allow campers. It is a time gone buy. It was a fellowship or fraternity of "meat" fisherman. Shunned by sport fishermen (true sport fishing purists, in fact the majority of fisherman, don't believe in killing large fish) and surf fisherman, misunderstood by regular people, the trophy fisherman and fish salesmen formed a closed group.

The biggest impact of Terry's addiction to fishing was at his job. While he never missed work, in the end, like all drugs, fishing began to take its toll in conspicuous ways. Or, better put, Terry's "underwear began showing." One time, for example, he fished all night, as he often did, and drove straight to work. He was early. A custodian let him in, and Terry entered his classroom and crawled under his desk to grab some shuteye. Terry did not hear the morning -bell ring. As students entered the class Terry remained curled up under his desk. Not finding him, the students contacted the principal's office and Terry's name blared out over the p.a. system. They checked the teachers' lounge, but no Terry. Finally, a student looked under the desk and found Terry sound asleep. He had already been given several write-ups for smelling like fish. Once he was caught sleeping in a closet. If you remember from my own personal experience, smelling like fish in any work environment is almost always a deal breaker. It also can be a relationship crusher: I met a girl once who told me she was dating a guy who cleaned fish for a living at a fish market. He made good money and she was in love with him but he always smelled like fish. They tried everything to rid him of the fish smell. A simple shower does not get rid of the aroma that comes from working with fish all day, and there is no magic soap or ointment. It becomes a part of you. Because he made good money, the guy did not want to quit, and she hung in there with him but after a while she began to smell like fish! This was the straw that broke the camel's back, and you can't blame her for it.

Jamie, in his early twenties and a former student of Terry's, loved to fish as much as he did. On the fateful day in November it was very rough, with a southeast swell. Going out in rough seas in his little Whaler was nothing new to Terry. On that day friends warned him, but he replied as he always did. Boston Whalers were unsinkable, which is true. (Remember, too, that the price for bass, still in the area and feasting on herring, was up that day to around three dollars a pound, an irresistible incentive for Terry.) But as he was about to find out, Whalers are not unflippable, and fifty-degree water is nothing to play around in. (At sixty degrees hypothermia starts after ten minutes).

The hurricane season was late that year and a storm out at sea near Bermuda was pushing huge swells onto Long Island beaches. According to Jamie, some of the swells were breaking early, about fifty yards off the beach. In the day time Surfers in wetsuits were all around Turtle Cove and the lighthouse. The night of the incident Terry noticed that, due to heavy rain from a Northeaster, another boat was taking on water at the Marina and was close to sinking. He called the owners of the marina and they came down. As Terry was getting into his own boat to go out and fish, the owners asked why Terry was going out in such awful weather, and that "they did not want to have to come down and identify his body." Always cheerful Terry gave his standard answer: "Don't worry, guys, Boston Whalers are unsinkable."

After catching several fish off shore in relatively safe waters, knowing that Jamie wanted to try casting for fish in the whitewash, Terry brought the kid in close to the breakers and instructed him to cast in behind the crashing waves where the bass had corralled the disoriented herring. The sun had just gone down, it was dusk and the bite would be on. Terry had done this many times before. While dangerous, a lot of big bass would be feeding in the white water after a wave crashed on the disoriented baitfish, making them easy prey. Terry would keep the boat in gear to stay just outside the breakers. He was very good at this. If he saw a wave that looked like it might break, he instructed Jamie to reel up and hold on while he ran the Whaler up the swell. Terry had done it a thousand times, and he had great faith in his two outboard Mercury engines.

Jamie was having fun landing fish after fish. It is possible that Terry had gotten too cocky, or maybe he was so busy helping the kid get the money-fish into the boat he did not see the giant swell approaching. After Terry removed a hook from a fish and put him in the cooler, he looked up and saw a huge breaking wall of white water ahead of him. Terry turned to run up the wave, but this time, this day, it was too late. They were flipped instantly and were thrown into the icy Atlantic. Terry and the kid both ended up in the freezing water. They managed to get back on top of the capsized boat; Terry was obviously hurt, gasping for breath, and he quite possibly could have hit a rock on the bottom. Terry kept yelling to the kid, "Help me get near the engine, near the engine." The kid was confused as to why he wanted him to do this. As he moved to help, he realized why Terry wanted to get near the engines: he wanted to hold onto them because he knew another big wave was coming. He was unable to do so.

This second punishing wave separated Terry from the boat. Jamie was able to get back to the capsized hull. Frozen and in shock, he watched Terry slowly get pulled out to sea with the outgoing tide. The kid made one heroic attempt to swim under the boat to try to get the flotation device that Terry kept under the center console. He was hoping to throw it to Terry, but it was getting dark and he couldn't see a thing under the boat. He groped about as much as he could, then surfaced for air and pulled himself back on the capsized boat. On shore under the lighthouse about a hundred yards away there was a lone couple waving a flashlight at Jamie; a beacon of hope perhaps. Jamie looked at the people calling for him. He thought of swimming out to try and help Terry but he realized the futility in that. Also, he just had a kid of his own to take care of.

Jamie took his shoes and pants off and plunged back into the water for the long swim back to the beach. Jamie felt his limbs grow slow, as happens with hypothermia. Our bodies start conserving heat for the vital organs, the brain and the heart. So the blood flow to the extremities gets shut off first. By an act of possibly divine providence, the couple on the beach helped pull Jamie ashore and got him to safety. If Jamie had not seen these people, or they him, he might not have made it.

There was much speculation regarding Terry's death. A lot of the cronies and pin hookers, devastated over the loss of their friend, relentlessly questioned Jamie as to what exactly had happened. But what allowed the kid, who was traumatized for years, to sleep at night at peace with himself was Terry's wife calling the next day and saying, "Son, I am glad you are alive. I always knew the call would come. I always knew the sea would take Terry."

An interesting footnote to this is that I was lucky enough to take Jamie and his son out fishing last summer. We had a nice time.

Yes, many men have lost their lives to commercial fishing. The point of the story, though, is that Terry did not have to fish. He had a great job that he loved. The fishing was supplementary money. Terry was addicted to a lifestyle. There was no reasonable explanation for him being out in those awful conditions other than the lure of money.

*

An Idiot at Sea

Everyone who fishes hard on the ocean has been caught in bad weather. While storms are fun to look back on with nostalgia, when you are actually out in one there is nothing fun about it. Here is the closest I ever came to not making it. I was fishing alone. It was a full moon in August so there was a lot of boat traffic that day in Montauk and a couple of boats and captains that I simply did not want to deal with. Jimmy George was out there with his spoon trolling all over the place, and I knew I would have a tough time getting a good pass at the fish. Too many boats push the fish down and they don't bite.

I knew there were plenty of big fish close to Block Island fifteen miles away, just beyond a famous fishing ground called South West Ledge. (I had landed a forty-two pounder there a few days before.) And I had plugged into my G.P.S what I was told was the exact area where Peter Vican caught the Rhode Island record (seventy-eight pounds) the year before. So I made my move and headed over. While my fishing instincts may have been accurate, I did not sense some low pressure moving through. The sky was blue, but it was not a crisp clear day. There was something weird about it. It was remarkably hot for Montauk, well above eighty degrees (generally we have only a few eighty-nine degree days over the course of a summer) and they had predicted thunderstorms. I generally like it when they predict thunderstorms, because that scares away the googans (hacks/amateurs/weekend warriors). If they say only a slight chance, or ten percent chance, of thunderstorms every googan goes out there, runs around like a maniac and pushes down the fish. Thirty-percent chance of thunderstorms is what you want to hear. Keeps people at the docks and ninety-percent of the time storms stay to the North and don't hit Montauk or Block Island. (Another free tip.)

It was flat-calm and my wonderful little Yamaha 4 stroke one hundred fifteen-horsepower engine was pushing my seventeen foot VIP non self- bailing bay boat at a nice pace across the sound toward Block. This feature, "self- bailing", is critical to this story. Ninety percent of boats out on the ocean are self-bailing, that is to say when/if water comes on the deck via big waves or rain, it flushes out large holes in the back of the boat. The tiny craft I was on did not have these critical drainage holes.

My boat was very small for this stretch of water. When it comes to bass fishing I have always felt, and still do, that the smaller the boat the better. I don't want a cabin. Who wants to be pushing around a kitchen when they are trying to catch trophy bass? I don't even like a t-top as they can interfere with setting the hook. I like a little center console and an engine in tight. An open transom is fine with me. A closed transom with brackets, while safer, just seems to be a pain as line can get caught up in them. Euro transoms take up too much space; a twenty-two foot boat with a Euro transom has the deck space of a regular twenty-footer.

As I made my way across the fifteen-mile expanse between Montauk and Block Island, I was very optimistic and excited about what was shaping up as a great night of fishing. But when I arrived about three miles off the west side of Block Island at a place one mile east of the famous South West Ledge, I saw a big, ominous, nasty looking cloud. My enthusiasm faltered a bit. At first, I was more annoyed than scared. It just meant that I had to keep an eye on the thing on the small chance the cloud would make the unlikely turn south out to sea toward me. Anyone acquainted with Block Island Sound weather knows that eighty-percent of the storms seem to hang to the north on the Connecticut and Rhode Island Coast line. They usually stay on land where they draw more strength. But this one looked like it had a rare southwest trajectory. It seemed to be hovering right over the entrance to New Harbor, Block Island, and had funnel-like lines that resembled waterspouts. To be honest the thing looked very tornado-ish in its composition. To the west and east the sky was blue, yet right in the middle of the sky was the beginning of a strong front that was liberally dispensing lightning bolts down to the water at a steady pace. (NOAA would record forty-seven mile an hour winds the next day on their web site.) The storm was probably five miles from me. I fished a few minutes longer before I realized that it was growing and headed right for me and a few other boats in the area. (One happened to be Jimmy Buffett's boat, "The Last Mango." I don't think Buffet himself was on board)

So, I started my little boat and headed back west to Montauk where the sky had been blue just a half hour before. I was about a mile into my twelve-mile trip back to Montauk when I quickly lost sight of the point. What was at first a clear view of the lighthouse and radar tower was now a white, all consuming, shadowy haze. This was not rain nor traditional clouds or fog. This was a windstorm. I had seen this before in Florida.

I knew the trip back to Montauk with its many riptides, was no place to be during a windstorm especially on a strong full moon tide when the wind was going against the tide. Waves are formed by wind pushing against current. Basically the rips would turn into breaking waves in heavy north winds. I was simply never going to make it back. That stretch of water had sunk legitimate boats in the past and would simply crush my little vessel.

The reality of my grim predicament was beginning to set in. A vague concern was turning into panic: I would be stuck in one of the Northeast's most treacherous bodies of water. In many ways Montauk, with its rip tides along its protruded shoreline, can be compared with a smaller version of Africa's Cape of Good Hope, which has claimed hundreds of boats over the centuries. My seventeen foot piece of plywood, essentially a bathtub with no drains and a four hundred pound engine/sinker on the back, had me feeling like an imbecile. I was just glad no one was on the boat with me.

South West Ledge looked exactly like high surf crashing on the beach except I was five miles from shore. Please accept that I am not exaggerating here. Huge waves crashing on a beach yet there WAS NO BEACH! At this point, the waves were probably five to eight feet. When I saw this I realized that I was probably not going to make it out. I was probably going to flip the boat and be in the water sooner than later. Just the thought of calling the Coast Guard was inconceivable. The wind was blowing so hard I couldn't get to my cell phone or pick up the VHS radio. I was hanging on, as they say, for dear life. I have driven boats through rough inlets and passages before. (Moriches, Long Island being the most treacherous.) I was pretty good at riding up the waves just enough so I did not fall off the front of it and dunk the bow, "pitch poling," as they call it. In some cases, if you get too ahead of a wave you bury the bow and it simply never comes up.

Caught

While I was somewhat confident in my boat handling ability, what scared me was the water filling it up. It was 5 pm in the middle of August. Even though the sun was still high in the sky somewhere, the sky around me was dark as night. But the sky was more foreign than that; it felt like I was all alone on another planet - a very windy planet. I must have been in the eye of the thing. I was drenched and shaking. The rain was pelting the water. I had the boat at full RPM's and I was only going ten miles an hour (I would usually do close to thirty at top RPM's). Would this sea let me out?

I knew I could not turn back into the waves for I would surely be flipped. Worse, I was listing hard to the port side. I could not stop the boat to see if my bilge was still pumping. I assumed it was not. All bilges have debris floating around: pieces of plastic, line clippings, bottle caps, sand etc. By this time something must have clogged the system. The water was right at the edge of the boat. The boat felt very heavy like it was laboring under the strain of a heavy anchor. Dreadfully, water was beginning to pour over the sides of the boat. It would not be long now. Even though I was under way, I was well aware that I was sinking. I would flip for sure.

When I first brought the boat to Montauk, I heard a unanimous cry of "That boat is not for these waters." One sage commercial fisherman took one look at it and told me that the free board (sides) was too low. Then he went on to very specifically tell me what would happen to me in a storm like this one. The boat would begin to list as the bilge filled up with rainwater. Then a relatively small three-foot wave would come over the stern and flip the boat. The engine would serve as an anchor and the boat would sink. The gunnels were simply too small and the weight of the four-stroke engine was too heavy. Once the air pockets filled, the boat would go down.

Everyone told me that I should never take that boat to Block Island, that it was not safe. And here I was. Yes, I was scared but I would not say this was my primary emotion. Remarkably, as is the case of all bad, bad accidents I am told, I got kind of introspective. It's more like an out of body experience. I felt the same as I did when I accidentally burned my parents' house down with an old space heater. It is as if I looked down at myself and the situation objectively from above. I was like, look at the poor forty-five-year-old loser stuck in this awful storm...what a schmuck. I felt dumb. I was going to end up in the water and might very well drown. People told me this would happen and it was. I thought of my poor mother, my father my sister, my friends at the marina. Oddly, I did not think of my girlfriend, though I loved her, but I thought of her dog. Her sweet innocent wonderful dog!

Scared as I was, I felt mostly melancholy, hopelessly melancholy and stupid- very stupid. I have always been a screw-up, a bit of a ham and I love to tell people how I fucked up, but this time it was not that funny. I mean, yes, there was something comical about some imbecile out for nice time fishing caught in a horrendous storm - although it certainly was not like, "Woohoo, this is going to be a great story when I make it home!" Those stories are meant for teenagers. The older one gets the less amusing they are. I could not handle another loser story.

Last winter in a state of deep depression, I entertained the idea of dying specifically this way, in a storm at sea with dignity rather than how it will most likely end up with me in a renovated basement with a coke whore. Like all addicts I need action. When I was not fishing and selling fish and not booking charters, I went through a state of being very depressed. I felt hopeless and useless, with no wife and kids or career to speak of and the looming prospect of the court case surrounding Andy and possible jail time. I occasionally entertained the idea of suicide. (Suicidal ideation it is called and apparently it's quite common.) I often entertained the thought of drowning myself at sea. After all, if you are "a man of the sea" like me what a noble way to go.

I derived very specific plans. One particularly gruesome plan was to pull up a lobster pot, like the ones that I used to unhook Jimmy George's lures from, tie myself to it and throw it over with me attached. This, however, was a mean thing to do to the poor lobsterman who would find me. So I scratched that idea. Another was to somehow swim up to the back of the boat from under water while the engine was running and hit myself in the head with the moving prop. That would do the job for sure, but who has the guts for that? Another idea was to catch a small mako shark (I guess a big one would do, too) and allow it to bite my hand allowing me to gracefully bleed to death with dignity on the high seas. To die with honor like my great ancestors. Or better yet, this exact situation that I found myself in now! All I had to do was bring myself to fall over the side of the boat in this horrendous storm (though I had heard drowning is a horrifically painful death.) This way I would die heroically! My Mommy could say, "Well, he died doing what he loved. He was a sea captain! He came from a long line of sea captains."

This is actually true. I am truly a documented legal sea captain like my ancestors. My boat is a registered commercial boat. My permit number is ny2279. My family name, Merick, is all over Yarmouth, Massachusetts. Our ancestors were proper whalers and owned/operated a whale processing plant over two hundred years ago. With that said, these pioneers of industry would no doubt be disgraced by my filthy little poaching operation. "And the womb of the sea," my mom would continue at my funeral, "The womb of our ancestors, the womb of the generous sea opened its gracious arms and took Jeff back." You get the picture.

My wonderful Mommy would say all this at my funeral. Out in this storm, my boat failing, I really believed she would say these things and really take solace in it. And let's face it; this noble ending would be far, far better than the way I will probably die, sweating it out in an un-air-conditioned room in Queens, NY.

Here I was in the heart of a very nasty storm, at South West Ledge where the chart warns, "Breaks in High Seas." I had my chance to go out with a shred of dignity. All I had to do was turn the little boat sideways and it would flip. No one would question it. Who would? The odds of someone surviving a storm like this in a non-self-bailing boat are remote at best. They would probably never find me; yet, as infinite as the sea appears, somehow they always find your body, don't they? And it is never pretty, all bloated and puffy. Somehow one limb is twisted behind your body like a pretzel. One eye has been plucked out by a seagull. As wonderful and final and generous as the outgoing tide is, everyone forgets about the incoming tide that inevitably pushes swollen bodies back. I imagine the outgoing tide was the tide good old Spalding Gray, the wonderful writer and performer, imagined when he threw himself off the *Staten Island Ferry* one cold January night. Spalding may have imagined the sea calmly ushering his body out to some distant frontier. But most of us do not understand how tides work; how cruel they can be. We never imagine our body pushing back up on the shoreline one hundred yards on Myrtle Beach, South Carolina, where some seventy-five-year-old man with oversized New Balance sneakers and a metal detector finds it.

But somehow, with the moment in hand, I did not seize the opportunity that I had fantasized about all winter. I did not throw myself over the side to an honorable death at sea! Instead this thing called a "will to live" kicked in. It is a stubborn little thing. No matter how big a loser one is - and a forty-five year old man selling fish out his van is pretty high up there on the loser pole - the will to live takes over. I wanted to survive. I wanted to catch a sixty- pound fish. I loved dog walking in Manhattan in the wintertime. I did not want to die. I was enjoying myself in Montauk. I also thought there was a chance if I ever inherited money, I could fuck that Russian chick I fucked five years ago when I was relatively rich from my movie/book deal.

I digress. I knew enough about the ocean and waves to realize that if I could somehow push out beyond the rips and get into deeper water (one hundred plus feet) where the waves weren't breaking, I might be able to stop the boat, open the hatch to the bilge and unclog the bilge pump and then start to bail the boat out with my hand pump and bucket. After that I might regain some sense of control. As it was, I was drenched and shaking so hard there was no way I could even pick up the phone or radio.

I kept going south to deeper water. I had to get off South West Ledge where it was only twenty-five feet deep and massive amounts of water pulled over the top of the ledge caused huge waves, and steep gullies. I needed to head to deeper water. I knew this. But the engine was at near maximum RPMs (5500) and I was only moving just ahead of the tide ("in irons" is the nautical term for this) with it going full blast. I might have been going two miles per hour. I was afraid I would run out of gas. If this happened I would definitely flip. I had the throttle "in the corner," or wide open, but I was barely moving, making no headway against the giant unyielding current. I was certain that I was not going to make it out.

Never had I felt so eerily alone. It was like I was on another planet and this was the alien weather. I felt like I should have been in a space suit. The wind was ridiculous. I was a steady forty-miles an hour. I did put on a life preserver earlier but now as conditions worsened I could not let go of the helm. The boat was listing so hard to port I could tell it was inches from flipping. Like on a sunfish sailboat, I leaned to one side of the tiny craft to try to keep it from flipping. I kept one hand on the wheel and, with the throttle full bore, tried to stay on course.

Eventually, mercifully, the South West Ledge rips let me out of their grasp and I limped toward deeper water. It is at this point that I thought I was going to make it. Later I was to find that the dimensions of the storm were small, only two miles long at most, and I was in the eye of it. Finally the waves stopped breaking. I stopped the boat. The sides at the highest point of the bow might have been three inches above water; the rest of the boat was at or below the water line. Water was still lapping in. A few more waves, or just one more big wave while I was not moving, would surely sink her. I carefully, gingerly sat down on the deck opened the hatch to the bilge pump and began to pull debris (wrappers, line, leaves, paper) out from the clogged bilge pump.

It was magic to my ears when I heard the pump begin to gurgle and churn and suck again. It was my friend. We were going to make it. I then took my hand pump and bucket and went to work. Ten minutes in I felt the boat become more buoyant. The wind was still howling and I was still in a precarious spot but I kept working. A mere twenty minutes later the boat was dry.

The rain and wind had dropped some. I was able to make the call to the Coast Guard on my cell phone. I felt confident that I would survive and could probably make it to Block Island Old Harbor, but I needed to know what the storm was doing. It did not look like it was going to pass quickly. Was there another front behind it? I was also concerned I had used up a lot of my gas battling the rips.

There is a process when you call the Coast Guard. They connect you first to Rhode Island and they take your GPS number. Rhode Island asks the basics: how many people on board, what port you came out of, etc. Then they have someone call you back. (I think this is how it went anyway.) Somehow the Montauk Coast Guard station called me on the radio. Apparently friends had reported me missing. I told them that I was not sinking. They asked me if I needed them to get me. Being a complete people pleaser, I looked at the lightning bolts and said, "No, please don't. There is far too much lightning out here. It is too dangerous." The idea of sending kids out to save my old, drug-addled ass was too much for me to bear. But then my cell phone rang and I was told that a boat from Port Judith, Rhode Island, was headed out to get me. That was at least twenty-five miles away.

Finding a small boat in a storm is not easy. Yes, the Coast Guard boat from Port Judith had radar, but in high seas with breaking waves looking for me was very much like a needle in a haystack. As it turned out I had to run up to them. A nice group of kids in the small Coast Guard craft (more like a raft) escorted me to the mouth of Old Harbor, where I immediately ran out of gas. I sputtered to a dock. They tied me up and then they were on their way back to the mainland. I was now on my own at the mercy of the island. Now you would think I would be thrilled I had escaped the jaws of death. I should have kissed the sand and run around shouting hallelujah. Instead I was more resigned - like, okay, I guess I am going to be on this planet a while longer after all.

But, as it turned out, without immediate access to any money as I had left my wallet and car keys hidden at the marina, I was thunderstruck. There I was, dead broke. It was 11:30 at night. My cell phone was dead and I had no charger. Now on my best day I look I look like a creepy, old, drug addict. If you saw me walking on the streets of New York you would say, "There's no way that guy does not live in a rent controlled apartment he inherited from his mom," or at least some kind of structured living situation like a group home. I have gaunt, sunken cheeks, many wrinkles from sun exposure and drug abuse in my twenties, and a big old honker of a nose. While I am often tan from days at sea, it is not a nice healthy fresh tan as if I just got back from a week In the Virgin Islands. Rather I have that reddish sheen, the pushing-around-a-shopping-cart-collecting-cans-and-living-under-a-bridge tan. You know the one. I have always had hygiene that can only be described as horrific. To compound things, I had been coming off a full moon cycle of fishing every day and night in the same clothes.

I must have smelled like a dead flounder. When fishing the full moon and the fishing is crazy I don't change my shirt, ever. My primary bait is live eels. Eels have a white slime on them that is a thick white film coating and on a dark blue T-shirt or any shirt really, including white - there is no nice way to say it - it looks like cum (human semen). There, I said it. In fact it looks exactly like cum, and it does not look like anything else. It does not look like glue or paint or putty. Worse is when the eel slime ends up on my shirt, directly at the bellybutton.

Stay with me here. When I put the eel on the hook, a particularly barbaric act in its own right, I usually use a towel or rag or paper towel. But during the course of the trip the towels inevitably get wet and become ineffective at holding the slippery elusive eels. So, when the bite is on, being in a perpetual frantic state to catch a world class fish, I have to find something dry to hold the slippery eel still so I can impale the hook through its lower jaw and through the roof of its mouth. That something is usually my shirt. I hold the bottom of my t-shirt out with my hand, pick up the eel bucket with the other hand, grab the eel out of the bucket with my hand under the shirt and then put the eel on the hook. By the end of the night I have white hardened slime all over both front my lower part of my shirt and the front of my pants.

It really does look exactly like cum. I am always so caught up in the excitement of fishing I never think of this. It never crosses my mind how I appear. I guess I assume everyone knows it is eel slime and I also assume they also realize that I often used my shirt to put the eel on the hook. But in reality most people know none of this. They do not know I used my shirt as a device to impale eels on hooks while fishing. Why would they? Now that I think about it, eighty-percent of the people I see at the marina and around town do not know what that is.

For years I have climbed out of various hovels (cabins, trucks, vans, cars) and proudly walked down the docks. People must have looked at my shirt and said to themselves or their wives, "What a disgusting vile pig of a man he is."

So anyway, I walked up to this taxi. I was soaking wet and shivering. I told the guy my situation. The driver, a nice man, probably the only nice person I encountered on that godforsaken island of wind-blown miscreants, believed my story. It seemed that he had heard about the search and rescue on the radio. He not only gave me a free ride to a bed and breakfast. He let me make phone call on his personal cell.

I called my friend and editor Dan Rosengarten in Manhattan; I told Dan that I was in trouble and to stand buy the phone and prepare for the inn proprietor or someone to call him so he can pay. (Dan is a solid friend, and he knew I would pay him back.) Well, a tired but not entirely unpleasant woman, let me in, directed me to a room and said that we would take care of billing in the a.m.

I could not help but think that I would have been treated better in days gone by, say Melville's time. I mean, the fact is, I am sure I fit under the wide spectrum of "castaway" by some definition anyway. No, I am not Tom Hanks or Robinson Crusoe, but imagine some whaler washed up on up on Nantucket Island after barely surviving a shipwreck? He would be consoled and fed soup, no? So with no fanfare I went to my appointed room. I must admit it was a wonderful huge house. I was on the third floor. I took a grand shower, climbed into bed and stared at the ceiling for five hours wondering what the fuck had happened. I don't think I slept at all.

When it got a little light around 5 a.m., I walked two miles down to the docks to check on my boat and the lines. It looked okay. I tried to chat it up with some other captains who were milling about; they were not real warm but I had no problem with them. What did I expect? I was a New Yorker. I wondered if they had heard about the pending court case with Andy.

I came back to the bed and breakfast around 8 am and I don't know why but I peeked into the dining room adjacent to the kitchen. There was a nice group of well-showered, apparently happy vacationers. One couple appeared to be on a honeymoon, two New York-ish women in their early forties I would guess, and older couple. Overall a nice group of people, they were chatting pleasantly it seemed.

Of course, I immediately felt that the nicely assembled aggregate simply had to hear my remarkably harrowing sea story. I was lost at sea after all. I was the one who was rescued at sea. Hadn't they heard?! Wasn't the entire island speaking about it? ...Even though it only lightly rained on the island that night. I survived a gale at sea! I must be the talk of the town! And here, low and behold, in amongst these common folk who were no doubt engaged in banal mundane chit chat, I walk in, amongst these pedestrian vacationers, The Survivor!

So I jumped at the opportunity to take advantage of this captive audience. After all, I was a performer. (I used to be a professional stand- up comedian.) I began to regale them of my adventure. As I was telling the story, they all looked dumbfounded but not as impressed or interested as I hoped they would be. I used to pride myself on being a pretty good storyteller; yet, some people weren't even making eye contact with me. Did I have egg on my face? Was my fly down? I had been in a seventeen-foot boat in a DOCUMENTED forty-seven-mile- an-hour gale. I was the subject of a search and rescue, to some degree, and survived! I was now twenty-five miles from home washed up on an island. But I got nothing from the group, just lowered heads and nods. The only reason, as I look back, must have been the white eel stains on my shirt. They must have been thinking, "What the hell is that! What kind of a pig of a man walks around town with that stuff on his shirt?"

Dissatisfied with my reception from the guests I entered the attached kitchen. There was no door just an open entrance where the angry proprietor was in a fit of industry trying to put a breakfast together (the second part of "bed and breakfast").

"Hi." I sheepishly said to her.

Annoyed at the sight of me, she bellowed so that all could hear, "Is your friend going to call me to pay?"

Some way to treat a man who was lost at sea, I thought.

"Ah, well, he is late sleeper. He is a comic. He does not get up until noon."

"Yeah, well, we need to take care of this bill"

"Okay, can I use your phone?" I asked.

"Yes, hurry up. I use it as a business line and this is my busy season."

Fair enough. I understood her predicament. I even liked her, but she was a tough cookie for sure.

Now, who to call? My girlfriend was either unavailable, or I was afraid to call her because that could be the straw that broke our fragile relationship. My comic/writer friends were mostly in LA and asleep. My fisherman friends were broke. All my Facebook friends were, well, Facebook friends and therefore technically not at all useful in the real world. (Don't believe me? Try e-mailing your "fb friends" and telling them you need a hand moving some box and then wait for the dead air.)

My mother would have helped but she was going through a period of tough love, rigorously reinforced by my stepfather and Al Anon meetings. This left only my father, a generally decent soul who was supportive of me, but he had put up with my antics for years, did not like surprises and was leery of giving credit card numbers over the phone. The idea of me calling him from a resort island in the middle of the summer and asking if he can swing for my bed and breakfast bill was going to be dicey.

"Dad...Dad...it's me Jeff.... Dad I got into trouble...I am on Block Island ...yes, Block Island, Rhode Island...I ...yes, the vacation spot...anyway I got caught in a bad storm and I am stuck here... Block Island...yes, the island..."

Caught

Meanwhile in all the confusion the inn owner burned her last batch of scones. The kitchen is filling up with smoke. A smoke alarm activated on queue. She is beyond pissed.

"Can you get to the point," she cackled.

"So... Dad, I was commercial fishing and I got caught in this storm and I have no wallet or money...pause...(dead air)...ah, so, dad, ah, can.... Can you put a hundred and fifty dollars on your credit card so I can leave and go back to Montauk?"

"Okay, sure," he said, appropriately sternly. My dad, as always, came through in the clutch.

I handed the lady the phone, "Hi...I'm the owner ...the address is 167 Shepherds Path...Shepherds Path! No, it's a hotel! No... I have been here for twenty years..."

I don't know why but during this back and forth, I peeked out and gave the now silent group of tourists a nice modest wave.

Then it hit me. I remembered I also needed gas money to get back to Montauk. I needed at least forty more dollars to fill up my ten-gallon can.

"Excuse me."

She was in the midst of writing down my dad's credit card number.

"Excuse me." I gingerly whispered, "Could you make it for an extra forty bucks?"

"What!" she screamed. The room was dense with smoke and burned smell.

"I need money to put gas in my boat so I can leave the island."

"Holy shit." Bellowing into the phone, "Your son wants me to tack on an extra forty bucks, and I'll tell you what, this seems like a scam to me!"

Well, a few hours later I got five gallons of gas and headed back to Montauk, where I was less disliked. When I got back, rather than friends calling to see if I was all right, I had a desperate call from Andy saying that he had to speak with me ASAP. I met him at the parking lot in town he looked thin and stressed out. He chained smoked.

"Dude, people are telling me that you are going to rat on me, what's the deal?"

"Andy, man, I am not going to rat on anyone. You're my friend..."

Andy just spoke right over me... " You have no idea how deep this runs, how complicated this all is...this is what I do for money, what a lot of people do for a living out here...do you know the only reason you're alive right now is because of me? Everyone wants to know who this recreational fisherman is poking around our business...I am getting huge pressure put on me, by distributors in New York...just do me a favor take a break from Montauk for a while. Your family has money; they will take care of you... go back to New York City...maybe come out on a weekend or two"

*

What Makes a Charter Boat Captain?

A friend of mine has worked on commercial draggers and long liners for years. He has thousands of hours at sea under his belt. He knows how to weld and mend nets, and once harpooned a 900 pound bluefin tuna off the back of a dragger. He is always giving me a hard time about what a joke the charter business is compared to commercial fishing. He looks down on charter boat captains and sees the entire fleet as a bunch googans with distorted egos trolling round pretending to be real fishermen. I laugh and play along, but in the end I know he is wrong. A busy charter boat captain working day in and day out (not like me) has to deal with a lot of frustrating situations that a commercial fisherman doesn't have to. Yes, as we all know, commercial fishing is one of the most dangerous jobs in the world, this is true, and they are remarkably skilled, hardworking men. After all, they have to be able to mend nets and weld metal doors and chain links often in freezing weather on a rocking boat.

With this said, isn't the commercial guy's job pretty straightforward? A good job has well defined goals and allows one to get lost in ones work. The brief time I spent on a squid boat I loved it. I found it relaxing separating squid and loading boxes. Simple hard work is good for the soul. Take a lobsterman, for instance. Barring the inevitable setbacks, and they are formidable, (especially on Long Island Sound were the lobsters have all but disappeared because of pollution caused by septic run off) his primary goal is to set the pots, then go back and pull them up. A commercial dragger in theory lets his nets out, and then pulls them in. Pretty basic. Everything is relative: we must admit that if a guy from a 1930 Arctic whaling vessel was able to time travel to the future and saw someone pushing a button and starting a hydraulic engine to pull in a net, he would probably scoff at how easy that is compared to going out in a dingy and harpooning a whale!...in the Arctic!

But, unlike a commercial fisherman who can enjoy the solitude, a busy charter boat captain has to deal with customers. A busy charter boat is in the service industry, and just like waiters at a restaurant they have to deal with the occasional difficult customer. And don't forget they have to deal with tourists who do not know how to fish. Once when I was a mate on a party boat and the heads were not working, I had to tell a three hundred pound, sixty-seven year old man that he had to shit in a bucket. I would rather pull up lobster pots than do that.

When the fishing is great and everyone is having fun, charter fishing can be great, but when the fish aren't biting or when they are biting and the customers screw-up, break gear or can't reel the fish in, then it sucks. No one explains the horrors of being a charter boat captain better than Ernest Hemingway in the first twenty-five pages of *"To Have and Have Not*." Now I would say most charter boat captains don't read, but I beg them to read this passage. Harry, the unlucky, protagonist, who runs a charter the boat in Cuba in the late 1930's, has to deal with a hung-over mate and a manipulative dope of a customer. The customer spends the whole time complaining and screwing up the equipment as Harry tries to cope without losing his own temper. At one point the man drops an entire rod overboard, and then argues about the price of having to replace it. In the end the guy stiffs Harry for all the money. My point here is that any commercial fisherman who reads this should have empathy for charter boat guys.

On a charter boat the captain constantly has people in his/her ear, "Aren't those guys catching fish over there?" they'll say as they point to other boats. "I hear captain so-n-so was nailing fish yesterday." It is constant pressure to produce. Then there is seasickness... I have been out when literally the entire boat is puking.

*

Stop giving them out! (My Beef with Part Time "Six Pack" Charter Boat Captains)

Most full-time charter boat captains don't like weekend warriors like me or the little operation I ran. And I don't really blame them. Around ten years ago there was a rash of "Captain Schools" that advertised heavily online, "Get your Captain's license in three months. No Coast Guard exam! Sure to pass!" The truth was that there was an exam, but it was not taken at the Coast Guard station, and if you failed one of the four sections you could take it over again. As I understand the "captain schools" are somehow able to narrow the questions down from a vast pool of something like two thousand possible questions to five hundred or so, making it easier to memorize the answers. They give practice tests that you can take online over and over again, so even if you don't really know what the question means, if you take the practice exam enough times, eventually you will recognize what the answer was. What I am saying here is that, save the chart plotting section which is interesting and difficult, (made obsolete by GPS) much of the course is basically BS. Yes, some valuable safety stuff is gone over lightly, but this could be covered in a basic six hour boater safety course.

Not only am I not proud of being a "six pack charter boat captain", I will take it a bit further. I am embarrassed, and most should be. It is really just a front. How could a guy who wears those short, dumb fishing shorts with Ray-Bans and a visor with a marlin on it look like a real sea captain in the face and claim to also be a "captain"? I don't consider myself a *real* captain. I consider myself at best a fishing guide and at worst a con artist.

When I meet a real waterman, like someone in the navy or Merchant Marine or a cruise ship captain or tug boat captain or a barge operator, the most I will say to that person is that I enjoy fishing and the water. And if someone introduces me as a captain, I will wilt, saying something along the lines of please excuse that this person is in the final stages of dementia.

I remember some poor girl I was dating once, a medical assistant, had framed her certificate and placed it on her wall. Now most things that we take the time to frame and hang on the wall have merit and substance, documenting and celebrating a milestone or achievement. It may be an advanced degree, a newspaper article pertaining to an achievement of yours, or a letter from the president recognizing an honorable feat. In this poor girl's case, she had framed a certificate to *draw blood* (at most a three-day class). But still my heart went out to this woman. This is what she had. I had nothing but empathy for her.

On the other hand, when I see some dumb douche with his stupid, six-pack license displayed on his home or office wall, I can only think, "You dummy." You took a fucking, twenty hour, crash course, did a bunch of practice tests on a computer, passed a test you memorized the answers for and now you're a captain??!! My beef about the test is that there is no practical application. They don't make you back a boat into a slip or even tie a knot. They don't even see if you can swim! They accept a doctor's note saying you are okay. To be honest, I don't know how some captains even get that note. One captain I know is flat out legally blind. He has hit other boats and also run up on shore twice.

Another friend of mine who got his license the way I did simply had very little sea time. When he was ten miles off shore and the wind turned northeast fifteen to thirty knots and kicked up big seas, he panicked. He made the, once relaxed customers, horrified by demanding that they put on life preservers at once and instructed them to look out for rogue waves. For the encore the "captain" deployed the life raft that was packed in a case on the hard top. The wind dropped out, the sea flattened and they made it home fine, the terrified customers demanded a discount, and my friend had to pay a thousand bucks to repack the safety raft.

I should talk, when I first got my charter boat license I did not even know how to properly tie a boat to a dock, and forget about docking; I would bump into every boat in sight. One time in the fog I had to ask the customers if they knew how to turn on the radar unit. But now after ten long years, I guess I am worthy of the credential.

My point is that there are men that are real, qualified captains. Michael Potts of the *Bluefin IV* out of Montauk, New York is a second generation captain; he has fished professionally for over fifty years. Or look at the resume of any captain on the Viking fleet (the biggest sports fishing fleet on the east coast); everyone on the roster has done nothing but fish for their entire lives. Carl Forsberg started the company in 1936 and it goes right down the line from there to Paul to Steven to Steven Junior - all lifelong fisherman, all professional captains. Or let's travel down the coast a bit to Hatteras, North Carolina and meet the Foster family and the Albatross fishing fleet. There you will find three generations of charter boat captains; they started their business before World War II!

I don't want to undersell myself completely. Sure I have some innate gifts that no amount of sea time can give a person. I am a kind, fun, educated and personable guy that people like to fish with. Along the way I picked up some knowledge on how to catch some big fish. I was a professional comedian for twelve years; I know how to entertain, to make people laugh and laugh hard, and that has real value on a charter boat. I am also genuinely interested in fisheries, tides, the topography of the ocean floor, and ecosystems. I also do not say, *"I hope yous all enjoyed the trip."*

As much as I would like to be perceived as a "professional" fisherman, I have a hard time thinking about myself in this way. I am just another weekend warrior, a googan. You will never hear me refer to myself as Captain Jeff Nichols - that's for sure.

*

Ain't Nobody Saved Me No Buffalo

It was 1985 and the yellow-fin tuna were thick. Just fifteen miles southeast of Montauk Point boats as small as eighteen feet, with eighty horse-power engines, were being loaded with forty to eighty pound yellow-fins .Then they would labor back to shore at ten knots, almost sinking under the strain. Unlike today, with size and catch limits on all species of fish, there were no regulations then. You could take as many fish as you wanted. You could also sell them to whomever you wanted: restaurants, fish markets, supermarkets. Of course, the flood of these beautiful and now stressed fish knocked the market price to below a dollar per pound. Many fishermen just filled up large industrial trashcans with yellow-fins and then headed home. On a good day, anyone with a rod and a jig could get in on the action at the Butterfish

Hole, named after the bait fish which drew these yellow-fins into the area to feed.

Incidentally, there are no more butterfish at the Butterfish Hole because large commercial draggers with nets wiped them out, but that's another story.

My friend was lucky enough to be out one day and witness this incredible bite. They were having a blast pulling in big yellowfin when all of a sudden someone got on the VHF radio and put a wet blanket on all the fun. A man had simply queried a neighboring boat over VHF channel 19 (the channel most captains monitor). The entire fleet was to hear this sobering question: "Do you think we are killing too many of these fish? Do you think we will wipe them out?"

A depressing concept no doubt.

Almost immediately, some idiot made this statement, "So what if we do? Ain't nobody saved me no buffalo."

This remark expresses a certain attitude that underscores so much that is rotten in our culture, from global warming to strip mining and deforestation, not to mention the gluttonous banking industry. But I plan to stick to the topic that I know, which is fishing – specifically trophy striped bass fishing. This tuna anecdote is relevant to the plight of the striped bass, because bass fishing has been so good over the last ten years it is almost inconceivable that stripers could once again be all but wiped out. But the sad fact is that if profligate fishing practices aren't brought under control, they well could be.

Hemingway was considered the coolest man alive by many for catching and killing huge marlin in Cuba. After the pictures were taken at the dock, most of the prized fish were thrown into a dumpster. And we all remember the movie Jaws. Frank Mundus, the man after whom Peter Benchley fashioned the rugged, weathered character Quint, used to have a huge gathering of people assembled at his dock, waiting to see what type of "Sea Monster" he would return with. After weighing in huge great white sharks in front of the impressed crowd, Mundus would then tow the inedible shark (like blue sharks, whites urinate through their skin) out past the jetties and cut the dead fish free to drift off with the outgoing tide. Frank would justify this activity by saying that the magnificent beast was now food for the crabs.

It was a time when ignorance was bliss. People generally assumed the wilderness and oceans were inexhaustible resources that we could use as a playground. Today we know that this is not true. In light of the complete elimination of hundreds of species, only an idiot would think resources were inexhaustible. Fishing is a great example: the waters off Greece and Japan are almost completely barren of all fish today. Sharks and giant bluefin tuna have been depleted by up to ninety percent. And cod, once the Atlantic's most robust fish, have been all but annihilated by commercial draggers.

State governments are now reconsidering hunting and fishing practices. This is all good. People have become enlightened that it is not healthy to "harvest" larger animals that are survivors and the top of the food chain in their habitat, many of which are females and thus reproduce. But today there still exist die-hard trophy hunters who want to weigh in the "big fish" at the dock for ego's sake. They are the striped bass "cow" hunters. I was one of them for ten years. I know a lot of these guys. They are my friends. I love them. Most are hardworking, funny, good guys. Kind people. But many are a little older, and they'll simply put away their rods and reels for good rather than throw back a big fish. Personally, I plan to take a picture and release big fish. Getting to this place was a process. Not being allowed to go out and catch the "big one" tears at the very fabric of what sport fishing is! All through my childhood I envied the people in those pictures holding or standing next to trophy fish. I used to stare at beautiful mounts of trout, marlin and striped bass. I wanted to get my own trophy.

For a moment consider big game hunting. Hemingway posed with as many trophy big game animals as he did with marlin. Today, though, we demonize that breed of trophy hunter. Like most people, when I see some jerk sitting on top of a big beautiful brown bear or magnificent elk saying with his smile, "Look what I killed with a gun!", I want the hunter's head to explode or better yet have the animal come alive and bite him on the nose.

But in reality, that man is probably much more in touch with nature, his heritage and what he is eating than most of us. He has hunted his whole life; his father was probably a hunter and his grandfather too. All his life he's been immersed in this pastime. He probably had hunting magazines as a kid. Secondly, while we (or at least I), have the idea of hillbillies running around the woods with guns shooting at everything he sees, most hunters are very responsible. He most likely killed the animal legally, as most states strictly monitor hunters (more so than fisherman) and require permits.

In his book *Meat Man,* John Holst points out that, unlike our ancestors, we are detached from what we eat, where it came from, who killed it. We have no idea what it is like to process an animal and prepare it for eating. We are so far removed from what we eat, the work it takes to prepare these animals for consumption. Just getting them out of the woods takes hours. Also before we judge this man you better make damn sure well you are a vegetarian. The animal he killed probably lived a good life; maybe it died prematurely, but rest assured he/it lived a much better life than the chicken you ate last night. That chicken was raised in a box and probably had no beak from chewing its cage attempting freedom. Cattle have it no better. And if you are eating farmed-raised fish, chances are they lived miserable bacteria-ridden lives too.

So, yes, I and possibly you would love to see that bear in the picture come to life and eat the hunter. Or even better a reality TV show were the man is put in a fenced-in-field with a bear. All he has is a loincloth, a knife and stick like Rambo and see who comes out alive. Nevertheless, the hunters in those pictures are probably hard-working, law-abiding people. I know many hunters. Some guys tell me that it takes up to three hours to pull a deer out of the woods so the coyotes won't get at it. He probably distributed the meat to friends and family. He spent hours working on this project for people who will enjoy it. Trophy elk and bear hunting are different from what I was doing.

One argument against trophy striped bass fishing is that there is no point in killing them because the meat is bad. In addition to being tough, once stripers reach a certain weight they hold a lot of mercury and PCB because the big ones have traveled up polluted rivers many, many times to spawn. Also the big stripers are obvious survivors and the top of the food chain. They spawn more eggs so should not be killed. It is very tough to argue against this. Yet I and many others go right along doing it, apparently only for ego's sake.

From 1920 to 1950 fishing was solidly a rich man's sport. Rich men hired well-groomed captains to take them out to the abundant waters off Long Island, Cuba, the Carolinas and the Florida Keys. It was convenient then, unlike today when one has to travel long distances to get to the Gulf Stream, to encounter tuna. Years ago, it was not entirely uncommon to have a charter boat come in the harbor with three giant tuna all over 500 pounds. Salivar's Diner had over a hundred pictures on its wall documenting these days. My favorite photo of Desi Arnaz (Ricky Ricardo) dressed in a suit, with a bunch of big tuna around him. Sadly Salivar's Diner, an iconic place in Montauk is now closed; symbolic of the dying fishing industry.

People really believed that the ocean held a limitless amount of fish, many of these fish, deemed inedible (this is before the sushi days) were simply thrown in the dumpster or used for fertilizer. The saddest thing is that, with the sushi boom of the 80's, today giant tuna fetch between ten thousand and a hundred thousand at Japanese auctions. In the 1950s, there was no market for these fish. Most were ground up to be used as cat food, and some were used for fertilizers for farms and gardens.

Nevertheless, recreational fisherman who fish with rods and reels simply cannot wipe out a species. While we certainly don't help matters by removing big fish from the ecosystem, the main culprit for the demise of fisheries are the giant commercial draggers and their huge, undiscriminating nets and twenty five-mile baited "long liners" that catch millions of pounds a year.

In case there is someone out there who doesn't know about the immense destruction of resources that commercial nets are capable of in just a short time, please read Simon Winchester's best-selling book *Atlantic*. Winchester describes how immense commercial draggers from many nations (US, Canada, Germany, Korea, Russia, Spain, others) descended onto the Grand Banks and literally wiped out, "mechanized strip mined," what for hundreds of years should be a seeming limitlessly fertile cod fishery. Once they began to process the fish out on the water, salting, filleting and freezing them in their factory ships, the end was near. Russia and Japan started showing up with four hundred-fifty foot trawlers, trolling along with huge open nets scouring the ocean floor. In 1968 some eight hundred ten thousand tons of cod alone were hauled from the sandy sea floor. This was game-over. No fishery no matter how robust could handle this onslaught. The next year the fishery all but collapsed. You could no longer catch a codfish on the Grand Banks.

Yes, recreational guys can put a nice dent in a fishery as well. In the seventies, while surfcasting people used to think nothing of filling the back of trucks with fish that they'd go and sell for pennies on the pound. Or even worse just let them rot or use them as lawn fertilizer. This behavior will weaken a fishery for sure and it must be understood that if draggers were allowed to target striped bass the way they targeted cod in the 1960's, the entire biomass of our national fish, the striped bass, would be wiped out in a few months. Am I sensationalizing? I wish.

Of course, in some ways, fishing is a wholesome activity. I mean, whatever happened to "go out and catch a big one?" If one is not allowed to try and go out and catch a big fish, then fishing as the recreational sport we have always enjoyed as a pastime will be completely changed. Catch and release is not the harmless solution one may think it to be (more on this later). The problem, as I see it, with the true bass or big game trophy addict is that a big fish is all he wants in life. In a very real way, he wants a sixty-pound bass, or a thousand-pound blue marlin (a "grander") more than a career, a family or a wife. The pursuit of trophy fish takes time, even more time than that ridiculous sport golf that has destroyed its share of marriages. And with new technology such as GPS and HD radar the sport becomes much more expensive than golf or skiing. That is where, as I see it, the sickness comes in. At this very moment there are guys who should be working or playing with their kids but are instead surfing eBay to get a good deal on a top of the line Shimano reel.

I started seriously pursuing large trophy striped bass, cows, in 2002. As I say, I think in my case I was compensating for something. I was not a great athlete in high school, as I mentioned I was severely learning disabled and confined to special education most of my life. Hot chicks had eluded me, and career-wise I was certainly not a roaring success. All of my peers had gotten way out ahead of me in life with "Things" and basically left me in the dust but… but they have probably never caught a sixty-pound striper! When I hung my first trophy striped bass on the scale at the marina (fifty-two pounds), while it disgusted a lot fishermen (those guys who think, correctly, that they should be thrown back), at that moment on that particular day I was envied and respected by an ever-shrinking minority group of trophy hunters.

Had I caught this big fish thirty years ago I would have been respected by almost everyone. When Frank Mundus landed a three thousand-pound great white in the seventies, thousands flocked to the dock to see the "man-eating monster." Frank Mundus was seen as a hero in those days. The movie *Jaws* had just come out and Frank was viewed by many as a defender of humans against predators. Today he is seen as a villain who in his life contributed to the mass killing of sharks.

In 2010 I had money. I had paid the marina slip bill off. Things looked good. I was happy. I smelled like fish and I was making money and having fun. Part of my relative successes over those ten years in Montauk was that I was focused on fish. I did not go to bars. I did not chase skirts. I did not party. I did not do cocaine. I did not play golf or tennis. I fished! I saw many guys start to get charter boat carriers going out there in Montauk then lose focus on that singleness of purpose, start chasing women or get involved in drugs. Those guys would eventually screw up somehow. I knew one guy who woke up next to a prominent restaurant owner's eighteen-year-old daughter and that was it. We simply never saw him again. My motto and mantra was to always "stay on the meat." I was starting to make money as a fisherman.

*

Trying to do the right thing when no one is watching

Nowadays I preach catch-and-release to any poor bastard who will listen to me. In any given year 'till now my motto and mantra was to always "stay on the meat," and it was working. I was putting fish up on the dock. I was starting to make money as a fisherman but then things started to get ugly for me in Montauk. Not only was Joey Boy on me about Andy's pending court case, but other charter boat captains were telling perspective customers that I was crazy and that I was lying about my "40-Pound Guarantee," saying that it was impossible.

Impossible, my ass! Some nights at this place called the "Pig Pen" we would have three to seven fish over forty-pounds. Many nights we threw them all back. At least three of my steady customers only did catch-and-release. I made the guarantee because I knew I could make good on it and I did over and over again. I think I did a good job of quieting the nay-sayers because I would post pictures on Noreast.com night after night showing my customers with their forty-pound fish and big smiles. People from all over, including Australia; Canada; Roanoke, Virginia; Charleston, South Carolina; Georgia, were looking me up and planning trips.

Caught

I really did not care what people said or thought as long as I was producing fish. But then something happened to me that I simply could not handle: catastrophic engine failure. On August 13, the height of the tourist season, with seventeen charters on the books at $500 each, the phone ringing and restaurants all wanting fish, my engine blew up.

I went down to the dock and started my boat at 2 am. A light came on and one beep (no alarm.) I thought it was my hundred-hour light indicating that I needed to change my oil. Ironically, I was scheduled for an oil change the next day. I ran the boat for a hundred yards and the engine stalled. I restarted drove it back to the dock. The next day Bob, the mechanic who did the previous oil change, and I took the cowling off. There was oil all over the engine and the oil filter was just hanging there completely unscrewed. There was not a drop of oil left in the engine. The engine was destroyed; the crankshaft blown; the pistons melted, etc.

At first I did not know what hit me. *Let's put in some more oil and it will be alright*, I told Bob. He looked very confused and pensive. He told me it needed to be taken to a Suzuki dealer and that it was a very unusual situation. I directly asked him if it was his fault since he put the filter on. He said that if it was his fault the oil would have come up in the first few hours not at over eighty-hours. Other mechanics backed up this statement. Believe me; I called every marine mechanic on the east coast.

This was a real mind fuck. I had no money to buy a new engine, four stroke engines cost close to twenty grand. It took me five months just to find this one. Unlike other boats I had in the past, relatively speaking it was a great fuel efficient, low emission four stroke engine. Mine had very few hours on it (close to six-hundred). It was supposed to go another three thousand hours at least - five more years! Even if I did have the money, why would I buy a new one if it could be sabotaged again? What's preventing someone else from unscrewing my filter again or worse? The insurance company sent a surveyor who confirmed that the only way the filter could have come off was by hand. Eventually the insurance company concluded it was sabotage and I was compensated.

This was a big issue. It forced me to look at things in my life on a macro level. Maybe I should not be fishing? Maybe "God" is telling me to stop killing these fish that are in trouble? All I know is that I was walking around like someone let off a pipe bomb in my house. I was literally stunned. All my joy and work was gone just like that. Later I estimated that I lost five thousand dollars in real charters. I call them "real" because I sent my charters to other captains' boats and got only a small commission. I had to get on the phone and cancel or redirect seventeen charters. Most were, to say the least, disappointed. I was basically taking away their dream of catching a forty-pounder at the "Pig Pen." They did not want to fish on other boats.

I went from loving everyone in Montauk to trusting no one. I could not get my head around the subject. I wanted out of Montauk. Though, I have finally let go of it to some degree; to the extent that it does not consume my every thought. Still, I would love to know why that damn filter came loose if it was not sabotage. Why did it come loose? I mean, if Jeff Nichols is a threat to your business, trust me, you don't have a business.

During the three-year span of the Andy court case my life was threatened several times. Everyone was paranoid that I would rat on them: restaurant owners, fishermen, fish store owners. I did not say a word, I know I entertained the idea of ratting on Andy, but as it turned out Andy himself finally ratted on one of the trucks he sold to off the

Long Island Expressway. On the next court date, in September 2009, Joey Boy pulled me off the bench and into a hall way, with characteristic understatement, told me that I did not have to testify after all. He said that there was not going to be a trial regarding Andy. I only had to pay a $200 fine. Then Joey boy walked off, down the hall, no good-by, no nice working with you...just a cold departure. I stared at him as he walked down the hall hoping that like the tiger in the book *Life of Pi* he would turn around and acknowledge our three year journey somehow. I heard through the grapevine that Andy pulled up to the trucks, sold some fish to them, and left. A minute later eight D.E.C. cop cars pulled up with guns out and commandeered the trucks and the unsuspecting bootleggers. In the end, Andy had cut a deal with Maffaro. I never saw Maffaro again. I heard he has a desk job now and stays back west. Three full years of stress and all I got was a $200 ticket! Truth be told, though, Montauk was a better place with Joey Boy around, in the end maybe telling on people is not such a bad thing. Kind of the fishing world's version of "See Something, Say Something." If we don't act we will have no more resources left.

At Princeton University there is an honor code. If a student knows someone is cheating, it is his or her obligation to preserve the integrity of the University and to tell on that student. As a result there is very little cheating at Princeton. Why not apply this to our ocean's fisheries that are in danger of collapse? Maybe the motto "loose lips sink ships" is not such a great thing to follow after all considering what's at stake?

Because of my boat being sabotaged, I did not fish at all for the entire fall season until a friend had me out on his boat in the middle of October on a new moon tide. I had a feeling I had a big fish on ironically because it was not fighting that hard. I felt the weight, but it came up fairly easily, characteristic of all big striped bass, and then made one modest run on the surface. Fact: fish forty-eight-pounds and better often don't fight that hard. The hardest fighting striped bass, in my opinion is between thirty-two and forty-two pounds. They are the "screamers."

We got the fish to the side of the boat. I looked down at the human-like eyes of the beautiful striper. (Striped bass are one of the few fish with eyes that move in the socket like humans.) The fish was in the high forties for sure. I said, "This one is going back." We snapped a quick picture and I watched her swim away. Doing the right thing and releasing the fish was as rewarding and gratifying as weighing-in a fish at the marina and getting on the board and magazines for vanity sake. Sadly, it took me a long time to get to this place.

Though I had a good feeling about letting the fish go (and also take some solace in the fact that over the years I have lost a lot of fish that got free quickly by pulling the hook), I felt a little like Liam Neeson in the movie *Schindler's List,* "I could have done more, I could have done more," he laments.

The story at the beginning this book ended kind of anticlimactically. I never went out and shot my tormentor, although the situation did get much worse. The same night the commercial captain chased me from the Porgy Hump he called my friend who owned the boat and threatened to sink it if he ever let me on it again. Then he demanded that he come down and turn on my friend's GPS so he could erase all the markings for Southwest Ledge. Then he went around and bashed my name to whoever would listen. This did not bother me, considering the source. Trying to stay in the game, I went on other captain's boats with my charters and took just a little piece of the money. I did a few of these trips, but then I got a call from one of the captains, an old friend, right after our trip. He told me "Look Jeff, I don't know who your enemies are but I can't bring your people out anymore. Someone just cut through the steering cable on my boat and smashed my electronics."

I am now trying to sell my boat and thinking about getting out of the charter business completely. So long my seven customers-. I try to humbly walk dogs in NY City for a living; things are picking up (literally). For now anyway, I have to look at a fishing rod as if it is a crack pipe...one cast and I may be hooked again. I have to stay clean of marinas and boats. I have to ascribe to total abstinence, because, as the saying goes "If you keep showing up at the barber shop, eventually you are going to get a haircut."

*

Conclusion

My effort at redemption and two cents

Why the Striped Bass faces collapse...again! And a solution

After remarkably being brought back from the brink of extinction through a courageous and hard fought environmental movement (captured in Dick Russell's book *Striper Wars)* only two decades ago, the historic striped bass, the *Morone Saxatilis*, once again, inconceivably, faces possible collapse.

There are four main reasons for this and, sadly, I have been involved, to varying degrees, in three of them: 1) overfishing by "trophy hunters" who keep large breeding female stripers for vanity's sake; 2) poaching and illegally selling striped bass to restaurants, fish markets and distributors; 3) the dreaded commercial draggers, who have now begun to target striped bass for their livelihood; and 4) mycobacteriosis.

Draggers alone could bring on extinction. As I have said many times already draggers alone have proven capable of wiping out entire biomasses of fish. There is no better example of this than the cod, once an abundant fish intertwined with the history of America (see Cape Cod), now all but extinct in terms of a sustainable resource. Today, with the cost of fuel, and stiffer off-shore quotas on whiting, pollock and winter flounder, the once overlooked striped bass is now a way to produce some minimal income for commercial fisherman who, ironically, due to fish farming and inappropriate regulations, have become endangered species themselves.

Perhaps the most serious threat to the striped bass is mycobacteriosis (or similar bacterial infections), a deadly skin virus that destroys the fish from the inside out. This skin malady with its unattractive red spots or lesions subconsciously or consciously has the entire east coast fishing community bummed out. It sucks. Mycobacteriosis is a completely downer to the striper fisherman, weighing on his spirit and soul. Apparently, the disease shows up on the skin last. It is believed to originate in the Chesapeake Bay that is polluted from chemical and septic run off. Also, the lack of stripers' forage, primarily bunker, lowers their immune system making them more susceptible to disease. Unfortunately the Chesapeake happens to be the largest spawning ground for the striper. I have seen a lot of it, and it seems as though some schools of fish have it and others do not. Most of my big fish were spot free, this is perhaps because they tend to swim alone. Some test have indicated that it is not mycobacteriosis at all but some other disease not as fatal or dangerous to humans – Fish with lesions have been tested for mycobacteriosis at The University of Massachusetts and none of the fish had the disease. So, apparently, we should not completely panic at this point, not all fish that have lesions have this mycobacteriosis-- all we can do is try to curtail the water pollution in the Chesapeake Bay area and pray for this beautiful fish and hope that they benefit from the resurgence of bunker schools making the stripers fatter and healthier.

*

The Striped Bass and the Monarch

Remarkably, despite the striper's incredible historic comeback, (inconceivably) stocks are down again and the fish faces some real problems. In fact, do to mycobacteriosis and over fishing the striper's very existence is precarious. In simple terms, as an ocean fish stripers might not exist in ten years. We simply do not know their fate but over fishing certainly does not help.

By the way, I might be the world's biggest hypocrite. I am full of double standards. Still through the process of time, I have become a better more enlightened sportsman and dare I say environmentalist. I'm an environmentalist in the loosest, non-active, laziest way. That is, I like to preach more than act. I only recycle when it is convenient. (Like a big blue bin sign saying: PUT PLASTIC BOTTLES HERE.) For years I drove a gas guzzling boat when we all knew full well that it and boats like it contributed to global warming. In complete candor one time in my early twenties a man paid me to get rid of an old broken down stove. I drove it to the dump but the dump was closed so I drove it to a scenic overlook and pushed the thing down the hill. It is probably still sitting there. So I do not have an impeccable record but at least I am aware that I am slothful.

Years ago however, I did attend a "Clean the Hudson Fundraiser" sponsored by the Scenic Hudson Society. (Scenic Hudson Society is a non-profit organization that along with Pete Seeger and his friends has been instrumental in bringing back the Hudson River from what was becoming a lifeless body of water to a healthier, cleaner river.) It was a cocktail party held at The Central Park Zoo Society in a wonderful room overlooking the park. To put it bluntly and crudely (hey - I am a fisherman), the place was crawling with chicks.

I sighed up for a Hudson River walk where, as I had envisioned, volunteers armed with trash bags (ideally me and the hot chicks at the party) would walk up and down the riverbank picking up trash. It was to start at 8 am in the morning under the George Washington Bridge. The hot babes from the party were not there, nevertheless, I learned a lot about the environmental movement/effort that brought the Hudson back to life. This is my great story of civic activism.

Though I am not a scientist by any stretch, I do have some firsthand knowledge of how vulnerable any migrating animal can be. We all do really; look at the havoc man-made dams have caused for the Atlantic salmon and American eel. Once, returning from work on a commercial boat, I was riding my bike down a stretch of Dune Road in Montauk when I was enveloped in a vast dense swarm of Monarch butterflies that appeared to be flying southwest. There was literally a half-mile of them. It was magical. The orange and black winged insects were so thick that I could barely see the road. They seemed to be frolicking and so incredibly buoyant. At one point they were so dense I had to stop. I was fully inundated in the wonderful migration. It was a truly magnificent experience. It felt good to be alive.

The next season I was living in the same area and jogging every day around the same time that I had experienced the Monarchs the year before but I never saw one butterfly, not a single Monarch. It did not mean much to me at the time but I heard later that the majority of the Monarch population died off that winter. The Monarch migrates all the way to Mexico and that year Mexico had had a particularly cold and stormy winter. Much of the habitat that the Monarch butterfly depends on to live in during the winter was destroyed. An estimated fifty to eighty-percent of the population of these beautiful insects was killed off. "Storms in Mexico devastate an already low population of the migrating butterfly," the *Los Angeles Times* wrote. While the Monarch population had regenerated some, the same stormy conditions are predicted in future, with high winds and rain blowing out much of the foliage that sustains and protect them. No one knows what will happen.

Parallels can be made between the striped bass and the Monarch as they both have predictable migration patterns. Aside from fisherman's (both commercial and recreation) seemingly endless need to kill as many stripers as possible, just the fact that humans exist in such abundance poses a threat to the striped bass. After Hurricane Sandy devastated so much shore area in New Jersey, Long Island and other coastal stretches it's hard to say what future concentrations of shoreline population will do to the environment, but we can see how the past has adversely affected striper waters. There were few or no zoning laws back in the fifties when middle-class people started to build summer homes on every little speck of inter-coastal land they could find. Then people started to move into these houses full time and the septic problems started. Septic tanks were rusting out or over flowing and leaking into streams that lead to the bays. Science really can't say with certainty that pollution causes the stripers' disease. Striped bass were fine in the 1960's and 70's when there were no treatment plants and sewer pipes simply poured out into the bays and ocean.

During the building boom of early 2000's immense new houses included "bulkheads" or barrier walls that extended lawns out into bays, wiping out critical estuaries that supported important forms of life, like krill and eel grass and organisms that depend on them. Bulkheads and docks destroyed thousands of acres of critical ecosystem. Equally as bad, according to Kevin McAllister, bay keeper of the Peconic Bays on Long Island, is lawn fertilizer. "Lawn fertilizer and pesticides enter the bays and cause algae (algae blooms) to grow and deprive the water of oxygen," (from earthways.com)

"Nitrogen and other plant nutrients from fertilizers create algae blooms that smother aquatic life forms in streams, ponds, rivers and even the ocean. In addition, a main ingredient in "weed and feed," 2,4-D or 2,4-Dichlorophenoxyacetic acid, has recently been cited as a contributor to contaminating habitat." (eartheasy.com blog)

This all make sense to me. Doesn't it seem like every dope in America is obsessed, more than ever, with having the perfect green lawn? Whatever happened to letting your lawn burn out in August? Would it kill us? Before everyone ran out and installed high tech irrigation systems for their yards, we accepted that the lawn would look a little less robust in August. We also were much more tolerant of a few weeds. Remember when dandelions looked good? Now they are treated like they carry the plague.

Toxins drain off the land thanks to high tech watering systems and enter creeks that lead into bays. The fertilizers spawn weeds that suck up oxygen and nitrogen from the water, eventually creating dead areas and brown tide. Add all this to rising water temperatures, lack of food, PCBs and mercury and it's no wonder that so many striped bass have red dots and sores all over them.

From my experience the marks on the fish are much more pronounced on the bass in August than they are in June. The higher water temperatures are certainly stressing the fish. Last year water temperatures off Block Island and Montauk hit 80 degrees on the surface.

> Water temperature may have an influence on estimation of apparent prevalence of mycobacteriosis in fish. The growth of mycobacteria in infected fish may decrease with decreasing water temperature (Clark & Shepard 1963); therefore, bacterial abundance and the ability to visualize acid-fast bacteria in granulomas may be reduced in fish from colder water. - John's Hopkins Study

So another question seems to be: will the Monarch and the striped bass somehow adapt? Will the butterfly find a safer place to winter? Will the striped bass build immunity to mycobacteriosis? Or could they somehow find an estuary other than the polluted Chesapeake or Hudson to spawn? (Perhaps the Connecticut River.) Will states get a hold of their sewer/septic /drainage problems? (And animal life like bullfrogs can return to our ponds and lakes. Remember hearing them at night? And crayfish, remember catching them as kids? When was the last time you put your foot in a pond and saw five crayfish take off? I recently went back to China Lake and while it is doing ok it has many more weeds and no crayfish. Even water snakes and garden snakes are becoming rare in suburban areas. If only dirt bag poachers, draggers, trophy hunters and illegal gillnets were the stripers' only problem.)

There is doom and gloom regarding the striped bass fisheries from Cape Cod and the islands. Martha's Vineyard, Nantucket and Cuttyhunk reported another very bad year for striper stocks. But there is hope! Off the coast of Block Island, a mere ten miles from Montauk, there is a two-mile-long stretch (or more) of beautiful disease-free, fat striped bass stacked up to ten feet deep. Probably thousands and thousands of fish between twenty-eight and forty pounds - cookie cutters. Free divers saw them and we all marked them on our sonar fish finders. When the stripers were feeding, the fishing was incredible, the best I have witnessed in ten years. None of the fish had red marks or lesions on them, no blisters or boils. Maybe this class of fish migrates further out into the ocean and avoids the polluted bays? I don't know. But it was good to see this many healthy fish. At this point when it comes to the stripers' future we simply have to wait and see, throw back the big fish, and go easy on the stripers next spring.

Most of my information is anecdotal. Much of what I know comes from sitting around the Montauk docks for fifteen years or so, chatting it up with commercial, charter and recreational fisherman alike. One recurring theme I heard year after year is that right before the collapse of the striped bass fisheries in the mid-eighties, when the commercial catch dropped from 14.7 Million Pounds in 1982 to 1.7 million pounds in 1983 and spawned moratorium on the fish, a lot of big fish were captured and killed by recreational guys.

Specifically, two world records were set consecutively right before the crash of the stock: Bob Rocchetts's 76-pounder caught off Montauk NY on July 17, 1981, a record quickly broken by Al McReynolds's controversial 78.5-pounder caught September 21 off the Vermont

Avenue jetty in Atlantic City New Jersey. One year later a series of commercial and recreational moratoriums were imposed across the Northeast states.

There is a loud outcry now that the bass are once again in dramatically steep decline, thanks to overfishing and a bacterial disease. Yet in the last two years, when many fisherman where saying they can't find a fish, no fewer than four state records have been broken, as well as Greg Myerson's new 81 Pound IGFA world record caught in August 2011.

The number of big fish taken in the last two years is eye popping. In January 2012 outside of Oregon Inlet, North Carolina, on a charter boat named "Rigged Up", 12-year-old, Stephen Furlough caught a 63-pound cow, a state record, but just a week later Stephen was edged out by Keith Angel with his official North Carolina record of 64 pounds and change.

On January 20, 2011, Cary Wolfe on a charter boat "The Badabing" shattered the Virginia record with a 74 pound slob.

And on June 20, 2011, the most infamous, mercurial and storied fisherman in the striped bass world, Peter Vican, broke his own Rhode Island state record of 76.14 pounds, caught just a year before, with a 77.4 pound monster.

This adds up to one world record and four state records in the last two years!

There certainly are a lot of big fish around. I remember getting guff from people at the docks when I killed a 38 pound bass to fillet and sell. "You should throw the big ones back," people said. I answered, "Yes, absolutely, but there seems to be only big fish around".

According to the Department of Conservation, well over a hundred tons of poached striped bass was sold in 2010, roughly 5 percent of the estimated striper biomass. Health experts warn that an adult should not consume more than two servings of striped bass a month, and pregnant women and small children should not consume any. One might ask: Who is buying this fish? And more importantly who is eating it? I live in NY City. I also travel a fair amount and I don't see rockfish or striped bass on restaurant menus all that much. Yes, in the summer "wild" striped bass appears on the menus more often. But a lot of the more high profile arrests for poaching bass have occurred in the wintertime. Those arrests were in January and February in North Carolina and Maryland. Where are they trafficking? Overseas markets? Cat food? Is it frozen and marketed as fresh in the summer time? Believe me if you drive to Ohio in February you are not going to see "fresh striped bass" on any menu in the state nor will you see it on the menus in Manhattan. So where is it going?

With some reluctance, this fisherman has weighed in his last forty-pound plus fish, though I would be lying if I said that I do not look back at those days of trophy fishing with great fondness. There is always catch-and-release, but that is not as pure an activity. Some of the people who practice it believe many fish don't survive after being released. Anglers who use light tackle often fight the fish for too long a period, exhausting the fish to the point that it will never recover. This is more prevalent the warmer the water gets. In New Jersey and New York and Rhode Island, using light tackle for the purpose of striped bass catch-and-release in August should be discouraged if not outlawed. Keep what you catch to eat and then move on to fish of another species.

Finally, during cold winters the striped bass migrate as far south as North Carolina. This has allowed commercial draggers with their huge nets to target striped bass in January and February as they rest offshore before they go into the Chesapeake Bay to spawn. This happened in the seventies. At that time draggers were known to kill thousands of big breeding females, most over forty inches. In the eighties, you could fish for five days straight and not catch a striped bass anywhere on the east coast. The activities of the North Carolina draggers coupled with seine netters on Long Island and archers of gill nets littering the coast line caused an eventual moratorium on the fish. This made it illegal for both recreational and commercial fisherman to keep a striped bass. The moratorium for commercial fisherman lasted for a few years in the mid-Eighties and was responsible for bringing the fish back from the brink to a healthy biomass. There are really only a handful of people to thank for saving the striped bass. Obviously Dick Russell and his friends, but also a mailman named Jim White who happened to have former Congresswoman Claudine Schneider on his mail route. He got her attention by constantly dropping of articles regarding the decline of the fishery and speaking to her staff members day after day about the problems of over fishing and greed. Schneider partnered with the late Senator John H. Chaffee, a Republican, and soon after they submitted house bill -4884. It was an act to place a moratorium on striped bass. When word got out that Jim was involved in this he got death threats from recreation fisherman and commercial guys a like; people too stupid to understand that this bill would lead to the greatest decade ever of striped bass fishing 2000-2010, when both commercial and recreational guys thrived.

New York State allows draggers to catch striped bass as a by-catch. That is, if they are fishing for, say, fluke, and in their nets pull up some bass, they are allowed to keep a few. The problem is that they once were allowed to keep seven fish; now they have raised it to twenty-one, but are pushing for more, which may give commercial draggers an incentive to target striped bass, pull up huge nets full of them, and pick out the twenty biggest while throwing the rest back dead. This activity is called culling or "upgrading." A friend of mine worked on a boat out of Montauk and said that they pulled up three thousand pounds of striped bass in one haul between Montauk and Block Island and kept them all. This was an honest guy and had no reason to lie to me. I must say that in the hundreds of nights on these waters I have never seen a dragger culling bass. But what's going on in New York State, which catches most of its commercial bass by rod and reel, is nothing compared to what is happening down in North Carolina where draggers are allowed to pull in two thousand-pounds of striped bass a day. Last year luckily the water stayed warm in Virginia and Maryland so the bass never made it as far south as North Carolina. But with this type of activity, we will soon once again say goodbye to the *Morone Saxatilis.*

When one takes into account the recent greed of fishermen in Maryland, who poached an estimated fifty-tons of bass in the Chesapeake Bay in February 2011, and what can only be described as the massacre going on in North Carolina with the commercial draggers it is easy to conclude that this once recently robust fishery will collapse soon. While these commercial activities have always gone on, it seems that now the commercial fishermen and poachers are much more brazen and defiant. It is hard not to factor in the bad national economy. Sadly, it has become easy to compare the USA to third-world counties in Africa who have over-fished their shores with nets to the point of literally having no fish left. Of course, many developed countries – Japan and Greece, for example - are barren as well.

Corrupt governments, inadequate law enforcement and greed seem to be three biggest threats to all fish across the world. Though I've been on the wrong side of the DEC in the past, I genuinely feel that they are generally above contempt and work hard at their jobs. Though it might happen, I don't think there is huge corruption in the form of bribes. But what do I know? The problem simply is that there is not enough surveillance. I never thought I, an old bootlegger, would be saying this, but in order for the striped bass to survive we need more cops! According to an article in *Forbes* magazine the entire NY state waterway system has only four conservation officers! Enforcement works. There is one Marine patrol boat in Connecticut where the operator happens to be a fisherman. He alone busted over ten boats last fall for poaching large amounts of blackfish. As a result the poachers, largely Asian, stay clear of his area and only fish the New York side were officers are not arresting them. Blackfish poaching is a real as cancer. My friend pulls over boats with 100 gallon live wells on them. What kind of recreation boat needs a 100 gallon live well? Some 21 foot boats have huge plastic garbage cans with aerators pumping into them. What these poachers are doing is keeping blackfish alive and selling at the docks for twenty-five dollars apiece. Worst of all; Chinatown only wants the small fish that are under two pounds because they taste better. Don't take my word for it; go down to China town on your own in October, look into the live tanks of the fish stores and restaurants and you will see under sized blackfish.

I do think that some of the poorer states welcome the revenue generated from poachers, who often see the relatively small fines as "the price of doing business." One marina owner on the east coast comes to mind. This person has been arrested at least three times for poaching fish out of season. After the third arrest wouldn't you think that the state would pull this guy's commercial license and take his boat? It is hard not to entertain the idea that the local state government would rather have the income that this guy generates via tickets than put him out of business completely.

*

Today they All Want "Fresh, Wild, Local"

I never considered selling the fish I caught until one day I was walking down the dock with a thirty-pound bass and a fisherman I know said, "Do you know that's about a hundred bucks in your hand?" At the time striped bass was going for thee dollars a pound and sometimes it would be as high as six dollars a pound. This is because there is a premium for "wild, fresh" fish today.

Today, most of the fish we consume are from fish farms. There has been a lot of media attention on this subject, and savvy consumers, especially those in metropolitan areas, are becoming aware of where their food comes from. Farming is at an all-time high. According to Paul Greenberg, author of the bestselling book *Four Fish: The Future of the Last Wild Food,* close to eighty percent of the fish you buy and eat in restaurants have been raised in captivity. That said, high-end, east coast restaurants need to be able to write on their menus and special boards: "fresh", "wild" and "local."

Walking down to the Fulton Fish Market, or the famous Seattle Fish Market, or any fish market in the word, is not what it used to be. The commercial boats, by law, are not allowed to bring in much if any local fish. Due to artificial fish farming, the reality is that commercial fishermen's livelihoods have become endangered. Fish farming (not necessarily bad, but not the cure-all one might imagine) and bad/ineffective regulations have ruined the commercial industry.

Though I was a deck hand on a commercial dragger one summer and witnessed a lot of waste, I am not an expert on fish management. Sadly, however, I don't think anyone really is. I am not sure if any lawmaker really knows what massacres takes place on these draggers. Books and TV specials speak to the carnage of commercial draggers, yet the by-catch laws still waste millions of pounds of fish a year. For instance, if a commercial dragger's nets accidentally come across a school of pollock (or insert any fish that is out of season), while dragging for hake (or any fish that is in season), rather than being able to keep all the edible fish and freeze them, or sell them, or give them to charity for a tax write off, Commercial fishermen are forced, by law, to throw them back into the ocean dead. Simply put, you cannot believe how many edible fish are killed in nets and thrown back dead. I saw it. It is mind blowing. Tons of fish. Anyway, I am overreaching my expertise. The point is: many Manhattan restaurants are willing to take a chance and buy fish from illegitimate sources, and I was part of that source for a while.

Unloading a few fish to a Greek diner in Flushing at two dollars a pound can suddenly turn an accountant from Queens into a "player." I remember the first time I dragged a cooler full of striped bass, sea bass and fluke into the back door of a well-known SoHo restaurant. They all buy fresh bass. By the way, any time you have seen striped bass on a menu in Manhattan, chances are it is a black market fish. The restaurants are in a difficult catch-22 position. If caught buying regulated fish from an illegitimate source, they will get cited by the Department of Conservation and face a stiff fine or even get shut down.

You would be surprised if you knew how many guys with good jobs and plenty of money, engage in bootlegging and poaching. They want to feel like hustlers. It's a high. A lot of guys use the barter system, which is a huge loophole in the system. In the "we hook 'em, you cook 'em" cycle, they dump a PCB, mercury-laden bass at a restaurant, bring thirty people in for dinner the next night, point to the special "Local wild striped bass" on the menu, and triumphantly bellow, "I caught that!"

Some might be thinking, *what's the big deal? Why not sell to a restaurant? Who cares?* Thirty years ago there were no regulations and anyone could sell anything to a restaurant. All this regulation stuff is relatively recent. In the late 1970s, netting off the beaches of Maryland, Long Island, NY, and Jersey decimated the bass population completely. Environmentalists – thank god! – pushed lawmakers, and put an end to this practice, to the great chagrin of Billy Joel, who wrote songs siding with the fishermen. In my opinion, Billy Joel should be going after the fish farming industry, as they are the ones hurting the commercial boats today. Maybe he is.

Thanks to the efforts of citizens like Dick Russell and his collation, Captain Jim White and lawmakers congresswoman Claudine Schneider and the late Republican Senator John H. Chaffee, laws have been put in place to keep striped bass a sustainable natural resource. They did this by:

1) Outlawing destructive commercial draggers (boats) from targeting striped bass and preventing them from catching thousands of pounds in one day. At one point in the 70s there was so much striped bass coming into the docks from commercial boats that the price of striped

bass dropped to just pennies on the pound! That is cat food level. Also, draggers off North Carolina found beds of huge female bass offshore and decimated the population in just a few days. It was actually President Bush who made it illegal to fish commercially or for recreation more than three miles off shore to prevent this type of thing from happening again.

2) Outlawing haul seine netting, where trucks pull in ropes attached to nets with thousands of pounds of striped bass in one haul off the beach.

3) Regulating commercial fishermen's intake from boat and gillnets (pin hookers).

4) Private boats could no longer load up with as many fish as possible and sell them to restaurants or give them out to neighbors. Now each state has fish limits.

Now that the market was not saturated, striped bass were worth much more than pennies on the pound. Striped bass were now worth up to six dollars a pound for the entire fish. However, law enforcement was lax almost to the point of non-existence in some states, allowing a huge black market industry to emerge. The following write-up in the *Baltimore Sun* shows how much money is at stake and that finally some significant enforcement is taking place. Previously, someone caught selling fish would be given a two thousand dollar fine, a relative trifle for many. None of the fishermen I was associated with dealt in anywhere near the volume of these guys, but it substantiates my point. Most bass you get at restaurants are illegally caught.

From the ***Baltimore Sun***, October 1 2010:

A Virginia waterman was sentenced Friday in the U.S. District Court in Greenbelt to five months in prison and five months of home detention for his role in the largest striped bass poaching ring in the history of the Chesapeake Bay.

[The fisherman] also was ordered to serve three years of supervised release, to pay a $1,000 fine and $5,818 in restitution by Judge Peter Messitte, who has presided over all the cases.

The poacher admitted that between 2005 and 2007, with the help of others, he poached 16,647 pounds of striped bass from the Potomac River and its tributaries. The fish had a market value of about $83,236.

These were fish pirates," said a high-ranking Virginia official, who asked not to be named because he was not authorized to speak about the case. "This was racketeering. Computers and records were seized. You're going to see some places go out of business."

"The watermen and fish dealers have been charged under the Lacey Act, which prohibits the illegal taking of wildlife in one state for the purpose of selling it in another. Violations of the act carry a maximum penalty of five years in prison and a fine of up to $250,000 . . .

One would think that such a far-reaching "bust" would be a deterrent, but far from it. Just this last February, Maryland authorities came across three hundred yards of illegally submerged gillnets that held an astounding ten thousand tons of striped bass. I repeat: ten thousand tons! And this was one tiny area of their vast spawning ground. God only knows how many other nets were and are out there. All we do know is that there is still a huge demand. Who is buying these fish? And who is eating it? Between commercial fishermen pulling in thousands of tons of striped bass a season and the estimated 60 tons of fish that poachers are taking, where is this fish going? Who is eating the PCB-laden meat? The health department recommends only two servings a month, even less for children and none for pregnant women. Some scientists are not even sure if it's healthy to eat stripers at all. Add skin disease to the mix.

So, it is an understatement to say that there are unscrupulous people out there with no regard for the health of the fisheries or interest in protecting national resources. While I was certainly not part of the solution with my little operation, I was never close to this scale. In fact, as I have stated, I never brought in more than my limit: one fish over twenty-eight-inches, one over forty. True, as I've also said, I did sell fish to restaurants. At first I did not even know it was illegal. I was eventually caught and asked to testify against other fisherman and restaurants on eastern Long Island. I was harassed endlessly by the D.E.C., threatened with prison time. In the end I got off with a two hundred dollar fine and no record. But I was never caught over my limit because, while I do believe the ocean can be harvested, and while I do care about the fishery, it was mainly because getting caught would be beyond humiliating. I mean getting caught with five striped bass over my daily limit is right up there with killing a bunch of bald eagles. It is sacrilegious and disgraceful, like selling cocaine on a playground.

We must protect our resources. In the 1980's striped bass almost became extinct due to the aforementioned reasons as well as the practice of beach seine netting; a practice where dories would pull nets back onto the beach (like Andy and I did), loaded with tons of migrating striped bass. Now haul seine netting from the beach is illegal but there are plenty of nets that are still used like fish traps and gillnets. With the increase in poaching (and other environmental factors), these fish face a real threat of getting wiped out.

Knowing that I am a striper junkie, well-intentioned friends or family members often call and tell me that there is some article about striped bass in the *New York Times* that I need to see. While I love and respect the *NY Times,* I tend to find their articles on striped bass a little, dare I say it, anemic and well... un-*Times* like. I mean how many variations of "fly fishing off the shoals on Nantucket" themes can they recycle? So now when someone mentions an article to me about striped bass that I "need to read" I say politely: "Thank you very much but if the article is not about A) mycobacteriosis and/or B) the estimated five hundred tons of illegal striped bass sold every year on the black market by bootleggers to be processed as cat food, I don't have time to read it. But thanks for the heads up."

*

Commercial Draggers

What I'd like to be reading much more about in the New York Times, or anywhere else, is the destructive effect of draggers. I truly feel bad for the operators of these boats. I am not unsympathetic to their eternal argument that they should be able to keep more fish not less. This is true to an extent. If stocks regenerate after the inevitable upcoming moratorium and that's a big if, draggers should be able to harvest a small amount of striped bass. But it has to be closely monitored. Many of these men are third generation fishermen. They are very hard working and highly skilled and they deserve better. For Christ sake, commercial fishermen know how to mend a net with needle and thread in high seas in 10-degree temperatures! Let them harvest some bass, but let's never forget how they wiped out the cod in the '60's. Commercial fishermen, a stubborn lot, won't recognize this fact. This does not serve them well. An acquaintance of mine captained a commercial boat for years (incidentally, his motto used to be, "Kill them big and small".) He recently looked me in the eye and told me that Greenpeace was the reason that the codfish were wiped out. I was shocked. He then said that the environmental group Greenpeace was protecting the seal population from hunters in Greenland and because not enough seals were being clubbed they ate all the cod, every one of them. It was not the four-hundred-fifty-foot Russian draggers but the seals that wiped out the codfish, according to this enlightened gentleman. This guy really believed it. Commercial fishermen in my experience simply cannot say, "You know what? You're right; draggers wiped out the cod." Perhaps if they took that approach then not quite as many groups would be trying to put them out of business.

Another big problem with commercial draggers is how they destroy the ocean floor. A farmer knows he has to take care of his land to get a good crop the following season. But the draggers mentality is slash and burn. Once they destroy one area of ocean bottom with their heavy gear, making sure no form of life will ever grow there again, they move on two another section. It really is that simple and that awful.

Nets have been used to catch fish from the beginning of time but as I keep repeating, the boats have become so efficient due to technology that they are now capable of wiping out the entire biomass of any particular species. Case in point, there used to be a great place to fish fifteen miles off Montauk called the Butterfish Hole. The butterfish used to attract larger prey like yellowfin tuna, but the draggers wiped out the butterfish leaving the tuna no reason to come close to shore. No one has seen a yellow-fin at the Butterfish Hole in twenty years. I was always alarmed by the "there is enough for everyone" pro-dragger attitude of the charter boat captains in Montauk, and elsewhere. Only now do I realize that many charter boat captains hold commercial licenses. I know one captain who runs a party boat but also runs a gill net boat. Also, his brother's friend or cousin might run a dragger. For these reasons you will rarely hear a harsh word against commercial draggers from the recreational operators of charter fishing boats -even if they suck up every fish in the ocean.

As for hook-and-liners ("pin hookers") a fish caught and released from a rod and reel has a chance of surviving depending on how it was hooked and fought, while a fish brought up from a dragger has no chance of survival. Pin hooking is the only way to harvest striped bass. I have worked with pin hookers. The guys I knew only targeted the fish in their slot limit which was no bigger than 34 inches. In fact, they were mad when a big fish hit their line. They had their drags locked up so tight that the fish got into the boat before it even had a chance to fight. I watched these guys throw back hundreds of healthy fish that swam away alive... after only a one or two minute fight. Also the pin hookers use down riggers when they troll; they only have about 50 feet of line out, allowing the fish to come in quick.

There are many groups that want to do away with pin hookers all together and make striped bass simply a game fish. That sounds ridiculous to me. All of Block Island sound has maybe 10 licensed commercial fishermen fishing for bass on a given night. The average boat, assuming the weather is good and the fish are feeding (big if's) will capture 200 pounds of fish, a red hot boat 300 pounds. This is not a lot of fish, when you consider that a dragger with a net could, in one haul, land more fish than the entire fleet of pin hookers.

This is not to say that there are not unscrupulous hook and line guys out there that allow greed to supersede their conscience. Hopefully these men are arrested. I know this sounds harsh but these men were given the privilege to harvest these beautiful fish- not to devastate the fishery.

Some of these accounts have been illustrative of just some of the massive waste that takes place aboard commercial draggers. Again, I am not a marine biologist or an authority on fish management but when it comes to draggers what I know is what I saw. It's hard to believe that any lawmaker who sees what I've seen wouldn't work to change the laws. There is a belief by many, including some recreational fisherman, environmentalists and even members of the Atlantic States Marine Fishery Commission that many fish that come up in the commercial nets that are off limits or out of season can be thrown back into the ocean to swim off and live again. I feel it is very important when discussing commercial draggers that we accept the fact that the chance of a fish surviving commercial draggers' nets is slim. Again, no striped bass or other desirable fish thrown back into the water after being brought up in a net is very likely to survive.

One option might be to allow draggers to target bass on a particular day with no slot limit. Have monitors assigned to boats. When I say monitors I mean real monitors, not some indifferent college kid that will look the other way, but good salaried D.E.C. officers, public servants in the truest sense of the title. Their entire day should be documented not only in writing but also on video. When the quota is reached, say, thirty thousand-pounds, they can no longer fish for bass anymore.

Commercial fishermen are often the first to admit that there is huge amount of waste in the form of mistakenly caught by-catch. They don't like throwing back dead edible fish either. It is nearly impossible to fish solely for one species of fish without encountering another species of fish that is out of season or off limits. For example, once I was working on a commercial dragger, fishing for squid and we happened upon a three thousand pound net of dead dogfish (or sand sharks). They had been crushed by the net. While considered a garbage fish by many, they do have some value overseas - but we cut the bag and discarded the fish back into the sea to serve as crab food.

Granted, I worked on a dragger for only a relatively short period of time, a little under one month, but in that time we discarded what I would guess to be eighty percent of what we pulled up in the nets. The only exception to this was the week we spent squid fishing twenty-five miles off shore. In those cases the bags came up with very little by-catch. We netted a couple of fluke, a skate or two, a few bass, but mostly squid. This was drag fishing at its best. This is not to say that the further off shore one goes the cleaner and purer the catches. Often, fish school and feed in the same area, fish such as whiting, haddock and pollock. One time a friend was working on a dragger off Maine. Haddock was in season while pollock was not, so he had to throw all the pollock back over the side, dead. In one instance he told me that they wasted well over two thousand pounds of fish. Some of this absurd and monstrous waste can be seen on YouTube.

*

Draggers and Striped Bass

I think some fishermen, especially commercial industry guys will say, "Well, what does this guy know about our industry? He only worked on two draggers totaling less than one month at sea fishing." While the point has some merit, statistics work the other way too. You mean to tell me that I happened to stumble upon the only two draggers in the world that were senselessly throwing hundreds of pounds of fish overboard dead? Out of all the boats out there I found the only two bad apples...Nonsense.

When I worked on a dragger off Long Island in 1998 we switched our nets from those for squid (calamari) to larger inshore nets intended to catch weakfish, otherwise known as sea trout. The weakfish, a beautifully colored fish, is named after its relatively soft jaw. The weakfish had to be sixteen inches long to keep commercially. For three days we pulled up and threw over dead probably a thousand pounds (or more) of weakfish that were between thirteen and fifteen inches long and not "keepers" and bellow the slot limit. As a recreational fisherman this waste horrified me. But it wasn't until the next day, when the captain told me that he was going to get his quota of seven striped bass, that I was truly demoralized. This was my fish! We pulled up what I estimated to be one thousand pounds of stripers that day. Once all the bass were on the deck, sucking on air and giving their last flops of life, there may have been a chance for some of these fish to survive if we threw them back right away, but in the name of commerce and productivity, the captain was more focused on getting the nets back out to catch more fish. I was instructed to sort through them and take the biggest seven bass. There must have been 300 stripers on the deck at one point. I was counseled to start to put the nets back out again. I worked quickly, hoping to save some bass, but there was no point. The ones I managed to throw over without the captain seeing me simply floated around in circles on the surface, otherwise known as the death spiral, while others lay motionless, crushed by the huge weight of the fishnets. Once we had seven fish, I began the methodical, awful task of throwing the dead fish over the side as the captain steamed off to find another school of weakfish to massacre. Some may think I am making this story up...I wish I was.

This practice is called culling or “upgrading," meaning picking through their catch for the best fish. While not illegal it is considered immoral and condemned by most. When we were fishing for squid I loved being a commercial fisherman. I loved the hard work and the *industry* of it all: the icing and storing of the fish in boxes and working in the “fish hole.” And being on the sea! What a delight, the breathtaking sunrises and sunsets. I also respected the skill of the fishermen; their ability to navigate, mend nets, find fish and fix mechanical stuff was impressive. The commercial fishermen I know are not thugs, as many of the recreational fishing community would have you believe. Rather, for the most part they are hard-working men. But there are exceptions and bad apples, of course, which brings me to a new topic having to do with one of the main reasons why the striped bass was all but extinct in the early 80’s: North Carolina.

*

THE Fisherman

October 19, 2000 - No. 42 Long Island, Metropolitan, NY Edition $1.50

WIN A HYDRA-SPORT 2390cc DREAMBOAT FISHING CONTEST

editor's LOG

COMMERCIAL FISHING BY-CATCH...LEGAL OR WASTEFUL?

We have heard for years about by-catch waste aboard commercial draggers targeting a specific specie. Here's another letter to further confirm the total devastation these vessels have on our marine resources under current practices.

Although these commercial anglers were within legal limits of the law, is what they are doing prudent? And, why can't our regulating officials come up with a solution to stop the mass destruction these vessels are capable of?

Dear Tom,

I spent the last month working on a commercial dragger a one-half mile off the coast of Fire Island. While I loved the work, and respect the skill and industriousness of the fisherman, as a recreational fisherman, I was alarmed, and shocked, as any sport fisherman would be, by the number of fish that were wasted and thrown overboard dead. Including thousands of pounds of striped bass and fluke, along with many blackfish and sea bass.

In short, the problem is that no real law is being broken. The "fishermen" are not keeping illegal fish, they are throwing back, as the law says, short fish, and endangered fish. The problem is that they are throwing the fish back dead.

I could see having a few hundred fish killed in the name of capitalism, but I am not talking about a few hundred, I witness nothing short of carnage, thousands and thousands of pounds of beautiful sport fish thrown over dead.

As the reader may already know draggers do not discriminate, they drag along bottom and pull everything in its path. A typical tow will yield 20 different species of fish. IE (shad, Spanish mackerel, bunker, weakfish, sharks, dog fish, porgies, kingfish, stripers, blues etc.). Many fish are kept and sold, this I have no problem with. However, it is naive of the government to think that the fish that are considered endangered or "off limits" are thrown back alive. Here is a news flash..."they are thrown back dead!"

My fear is if the government does not modify these ridicules, ineffective, limits, perhaps Long Island will become barren of fish like the waters off Japan are today.

I should also note, that I am far from an environmentalist, actually, I do not even recycle. I have caught bass using illegal short flounder. I say this to make the point, that the waste would have to be pretty substantial to raise the eyebrows of this particular slob.

While I am being honest I might add, being that I have never caught a weakfish I could not care if the entire population of weakfish were wiped out. However, I have spent too many hours trying to catch bass and fluke to see them pointlessly killed by the thousands is tough to take.

What happens, for those who do not know, is that the nets are brought in after hours of raking the ocean floor. The fish hit the deck alive, but in the name of commerce and productivity, all the energy is directed towards putting the nets back out to catch more fish. As the nets are being put out, the non-targeted fish are forced to suck on air for 20 minutes. As I see it, if the "fisherman" took three minutes to throw back some of the live fish it could make a big difference. Aren't these guys ultimately hurting their own resources?

My Question is who is to blame?

The commercial fisherman is not braking any rules. Does the government really believe that the 15-inch weakfish are being thrown back alive? Why have the laws at all? Would it be better if they were allowed a certain poundage regardless of size limit? I mean sure short fish would be killed but aren't they killed anyway?

In summary, I believe that the ocean should be harvested. There are, as any good recreational fisherman can tell you, plenty of fish out there (at least on the south shore). There is enough for both recreational and professional fisherman. I also know that most fishermen, including the guys I work for, while far from saints, are, talented and extremely hard working men, who risk there lives so that people like you and I can order fish off menus in NYC. However, speaking not as an environmentalist, but as a recreational fisherman, throwing back, hundreds of trophy fish, including many 40-pound cows, and 10-pound doormat fluke, seemed to be a waist. Am I wrong?

Some readers might feel that I am exaggerating; I really wish that I were.

Jeff Nichols

Managing Editor
Tom Melton

If the Fish Get to Carolina, They Are Goners

On a beautiful, warm and calm day in mid-January 2010, outside of Oregon Inlet, North Carolina, an exceptional number of recreational fishermen were out on small sports fishing boats. Slowly they started reporting over the radio and on cell phones massive amounts of dead floating striped bass (or what down there they call rockfish) littering the water's surface. Literally acres upon acres of dead stripers, many over thirty-pounds, had been discarded by commercial draggers who were culling or high grading, just as I had done years earlier off Long Island. This time, however, the carnage was documented. Everyone on recreational boats that day whipped out their smart phones and started to take pictures and videos. YouTube had postings of the massacre within hours. Hundreds of thousands of outraged people saw the videos of the sacred and historic striped bass discarded as waste. Hundreds of twenty-pound-plus dead bass littered the surface of the ocean. Now there was no more mystery with regards to commercial draggers and the waste they were capable of generating. Finally we all saw culling up close. It was not just one boat, it was several involved in this particular act of annihilation.

Luckily because of warm water in the north the fish did not make it past Virginia last season. But if they end up there next year, you can bet the draggers in North Carolina will be there to decimate the striped bass. What happened in North Carolina and what happened with the financial crisis in 2008 is exactly why we need government regulations and enforcement of regulations. No matter how moral a commercial fisherman is in all other areas of his life, you can bet that if he has big bills to pay, and if he knows that he can sell three thousand pounds of bass and there is a ninety-nine percent chance that he will not get caught selling it, he probably will. Regulation should not be just forms and more forms, red tape that the commercial fisherman finds himself flooded with; it should be enforced by effective monitoring and surveillance. Look how well the airline industry runs: all those planes and so few crashes. That is because it is regulated. If left unregulated the airplanes would be falling out of the sky left and right.

Remarkably, when presented with the video evidence the North Carolina authorities said that it was an "isolated incident" in which too many fish were caught in a net and the fishermen were unable to pull the entire net up on the boat. This begs the question as to why the commercial fishermen were using huge nets to begin with-if their quota was only fifty fish. Anyway, this argument might have held up if there hadn't been other videos of commercial boats dumping fish over the next several days. This was no isolated incident. Still, the North Carolina conservation authorities stayed ambivalent:

"Staff with the division is still investigating the incident but has been unable to confirm reports that commercial trawl fishermen were high-grading. High-grading occurs when a fisherman discards a previously-caught, legal-sized fish in order to keep a larger fish within the daily possession limit. While high-grading is not illegal, it is not an ethical fishing practice and the division does not condone it."

Finally, after a helicopter came back one day with pictures of acres and acres of dead bass, North Carolina came up with a plan to reduce this high-grading practice. They allowed the commercial boats to keep up two thousand pounds of striped bass a day, and if they caught too much they could call over another dragger to take over the excess. This certainly reduces the waste, but won't more commercial fishermen begin to target the bass? Also, this assumes that all these draggers are ethical and don't fill up with two thousand-pounds of fish, run in and dump the fish at the docks, and go out again. Also, this scenario means that there must be draggers hanging around waiting for the call to transfer a load of fish. My friend knew guys who worked as deck hands on draggers down there. Apparently, they caught their prescribed limit of two thousand pounds of fish, but then set out another net, and pulled in another thousand pounds of bass. The deck hands were instructed to cut them up in the boat on the way in. The fillets were put into big white garbage bags and marked "special order", at the fish house when the documented fish were unloaded the white plastic bags with the illegal fish were put just to the side of the documented fish.

During some winters the entire biomass of striped bass makes the outer banks its home in January and February. The fishery simply cannot withstand draggers taking out two thousand pounds of stripers a day, not to mention what is wasted. This activity in North Carolina coupled with all the illegal gillnet activity in the Chesapeake Bay, taking an estimated hundred tons of fish in 2011 alone, is devastating. Add recreational guys like me killing 40 pound-plus breeding bass for ego's sake, and it is clear why it is the opinion of many fishermen that, at this pace, the striped bass, the very fish that had seen a remarkable recovery in the mid-90s, will once again face possible extinction in the next few years.

The irony is that years ago North Carolina draggers were busy off shore landing winter flounder. They would have never bothered with striped bass, but because of the high price of fuel, and restrictions on winter flounder, the draggers have found it more lucrative to stay in shore and massacre stripers. The only reason the rest of the northeast dragger fleet have not targeted stripers, like they do in North Carolina, is because squid fishing has greatly flourished over the past decade. Once that dries up the only fish they will go after is flounder and PCB laden striper.

The solution: draggers should be able to harvest striped bass in North Carolina, but should not be allowed nets. Umbrella rigs with down riggers have proven to be very effective at catching hundreds of pounds of fish a day. Let them troll five umbrella rigs and various lures or use live bait off their boats to fill their fifty fish quota in North Carolina. NY State and Massachusetts have a very successful rod and reel commercial fishery. Enough is enough; there have been too many accounts and pictures of thousands of dead, wasted bass on the beaches and the water from nets.

To allow recreation fisherman and commercial fisherman to govern themselves is like asking Wall Street guys and bankers to play fair. We need more Joey Boy Maffaros, the D.E.C. officer who busted me. There should be someone like old Joey Boy in every port. Every fishing area should have one guy that everyone is scared shitless of. *Watch out for so-in-so, he will take your boat, put you in jail, give you a ten thousand dollar fine etc., etc.*

Creating a "division of marine monitoring" would also create jobs. Hire out-of-work or under-worked commercial fishermen. Pay them a real salary with benefits. From what I can see, especially in states like North Carolina, while over regulated they are under monitored. As it stands now, commercial draggers have no real supervision.

Yes, the commercial fishermen are being burdened with many restrictions today. This fisherman believes that the ocean (including striped bass) can and should be harvested. Why would such and abundant fish have to named a game fish? But as it stands now draggers are the most wasteful destructive vessels on the sea.

If a commercial fisherman is caught killing big fish and selling them illegally they should definitely lose their boat. This should go for marina owners who engage and encourage poaching as well. In Japan, if you are caught drunk-driving you lose your right to drive for life. As a result, there is very little drunk driving in Japan.

Marinas are occasionally at fault, too. The owner of one notorious marina on the east coast has been caught three times illegally selling huge amounts of blackfish. He publicly laughs off the fines as the "price of doing business." Why not make an example of this guy who is abusing our natural resources and encouraging his customers to do the same? When looking at this issue, one can only conclude that the D.E.C. likes the revenue generated by the tickets, and prefers that these poachers stay in business.

As for the recreational guys, it breaks my heart because trophy fishing is my passion, but no fish over forty pounds should be allowed to be kept. These are the breeders and the survivors. Let's leave them alone. They have a tough enough road ahead trying to survive with polluted breeding grounds, waterways with brown tide, mycobacteriosis and over building on estuaries.

Catch and release should not be practiced when water temperatures exceed seventy-five degrees. If you are fishing for stripers in these warm waters, take a fish to eat then go off and fish for another species. While organizations like Stripers Forever should be applauded for their efforts they do not recognize the danger of fishing for big bass with light tackle in warm water. This is a gross oversight. I was fishing off Block Island last August and there was a well-known catch and release charter boat using eels with light tackle. I watched them closely. Every drift all three guys would hook up. Every fish took around seven minutes to get in on the light rods. They were unable to resuscitate all of the fish they caught. I wish I had put a camera on them. They went through the motions of resuscitating the fish, but the fish were all going belly up. They, feeling guilty I would imagine, waved to another boat, any boat, to go get their waste!

The line of thirty-pound-plus dead fish following this particular boat had eerie resemblances to the draggers of the North Carolina massacre. Sure it was only one boat but multiply this "catch and release" practice by fifty boats...you get the picture. It is okay to fish for bass in warm water. Just kill your first couple and then either go home or fish for another species. And if you are going to practice catch and release, don't weigh the fish, put it on the deck, take a bunch pictures and then try to throw it back. News flash – if you try to weigh it, the fish is going to die.

Often fishermen try walking the line between protecting and returning a fish and boasting about the size of the fish. It really has got to be one or the other. Based on some videos out there it is obvious that fishermen often handle the fish too long. It is too bad. What could be incredible documentation of successful catch and release, videos that could serve as a "how too" for many anglers, sadly often end up as just another big bass dead. After many pictures and being hung up on a Boga grip scale fish are often unable to be resuscitated.

Only use a net on small fish if you are going to eat it. Nets remove critical protective slime from bass. Unless you are fishing from a huge boat you should be able to lean over and grab the fish by the mouth. This is not a bluefish or a shark. Stripers have no teeth. The large striped bass tend to roll over at boat side anyway. Make sure you use tight drags to get the fish in.

Finally, put pressure on your friends but don't preach to them. (Ha! Easy for me to say after so many pages of preaching.) It takes a long time for people to change their attitudes about killing big breeding fish. In the end they have to come to the decision on their own. Hopefully the government will step in and make it against the law to catch a fish that is over 40 inches. But with government cut backs, don't expect much enforcement in this area. Maybe some fishermen will look into the human like eyes of the big striped bass and let them go.

I used to fish with my friend Gary in Moriches Inlet NY, during the month of May in 1996-98. On clam chum we'd catch thirty striped bass in a tide. Most were twenty-two to twenty-six inches with a few keepers in the mix. Gary told me that when he goes to that spot now he catches three to five fish a tide and they are mostly all bigger fish - fifteen to twenty pounds. That is still a good day of fishing but there are fewer and fewer small fish around. This does not bode well for the future of the fishery. In 1998 the island of Martha's Vineyard was literally surrounded by striped bass. Truth be told, there were too many as they devour everything they can eat.

What happened was that nonprofits and government programs, trying to bring the striper back from the brink of extinction, created and founded hatcheries. This resulted in too many fish. The big mistake was that they did nothing to increase the baitfish (bunker, peanut bunker, and sand eels, in particular) that bass need to survive. (Ironically, there are loads of bunker around today and not as many bass.) Hoards of hungry bass in the late 90's devoured everything they could: crabs, baby flounder, adult flounder, fluke sea bass and skates; everything but dogfish. Perhaps this is why Jimmy George's Lure, the Secret Spoon, was so effective. The fish were dying to eat anything! So now the fish have been thinned out for sure due to over fishing. Right now there seems to be a good amount of fish left but I would say half of these fish have mycobacteriosis (or something like it). Any bass fisherman can tell you how prevalent this disease is. No one is sure what it does to life expectancy. The good news is that I have caught a lot of these fish with the disease and they fight very hard; many have a lot of life left in them. Also, while the cape and the islands all reported poor stocks last summer, this last summer (2012), off the southwest side of Block Island the biggest mass of spotless disease free fish I have ever seen were schooled. There were hundreds and hundreds of big healthy fish. Maybe this robust school will have a good breeding year. Maybe they will find a way to adapt to the pollution in their spawning areas like the Chesapeake Bay or go somewhere else to spawn like the Connecticut River. Maybe local governments will get a hold of the septic problems that pollute these areas.

What seems to be needed is another movement like the one Dick Russell outlined in *Striper Wars*. But can such a movement even take place now? It seems like no one even cares about global warming, let alone the health of striped bass. Maybe I am wrong, but it seems as though, as long as jobs were created, law makers today would have no problem with our waters returning to the deplorable state of the industrial revolution... were in the nineteen thirties our rivers and bays and estuaries were so polluted by factories dumping waste into them, no fish would dare to swim. The activism, which saved the stripers in the early 80's, took place just after an era when social and environmental movements really effected positive change (like the save the Hudson River movement). These were real passionate people galvanizing and augmenting a cause. They were also funded by nonprofit groups and environme1ntally minded individuals who may be reluctant to contribute in these bleak economic times. The state governments that got involved in hatcheries are broke now and the last thing they care about is the striped bass. They care about their jobs it seems. I actually ran into a big wig who worked at the D.E.C. We began to talk about striped bass and I asked him what he thought about mycobacteriosis...and he said, "What is that?"

There is already plenty of awareness out there regarding the dangers of killing big bass but little action. Some people just don't get it and they never will. These guys are an anachronism, from a different era. Even though ninety percent of the fishing community is against killing big fish, certain captain's egos are so intertwined with landing big fish they simply are incapable of letting a big fish go. Nor do they seem capable of any kind of activism regarding the health of the fishery.

There are also some people who will always feel a compulsion to sell their fish. I know a fellow in Montauk that always brags about how well his son is doing on Wall Street running a hedge fund. Well one he day tells me that his son went out bass fishing and "loaded up" on bass and sold them to a restaurant back west. I asked him why the son, a supposedly wealthy man, felt the need to sell these fish when he was already rich. He told me that his son was raised to sell fish and he isn't going to change. He, in my opinion, is incapable of showing any remorse for killing big fish or sell without a license.

Who knows what the striped bass's fate will be. This mycobacteriosis, a fearful malady, could be as bad for the striped bass as phytophthora infestans was to the potato. Hopefully some bass will be less susceptible to the disease and continue to perpetuate the species. Maybe water temperatures will cool, putting less stress on the fish. These hardy fish are now facing a life and death struggle and humans should go gentler on them, and respect the fish. The Morone Saxatilis is one of this country's last great natural migrations and a historically important fish. One thing is for sure; if we do not stop recklessly slaughtering the striped bass solely in the name of commerce and ego, they will go the way of the buffalo.

***

Made in United States
North Haven, CT
26 July 2022

21832388R00125